OWN IT! 4

B1 Preliminary test content in Own It! Level 4 has been checked by Cambridge Assessment English for accuracy and level.

STUDENT'S BOOK
WITH PRACTICE EXTRA

Samantha Lewis and Daniel Vincent
with Andrew Reid

CAMBRIDGE
UNIVERSITY PRESS

CONTENTS

	Vocabulary	Language in action	Reading
Unit 5 **Wonderful world** p58	Processes p59 Extreme adjectives p62	The passive p61 Question tags and questions with prepositions p63	A webzine article: Smart cities of the future p60 A travel blog: Scott the Explorer p66 Extreme homes p66
Unit review p68, **Finished?** p122			
Unit 6 **No limits** p70	Verb collocations with *get*, *take* and *have* p71 Inspiration and challenge p74	First and second conditional p73 Third conditional p75	A fact sheet: When taking risks is a good thing p72 Citizenship: Digital Citizenship: case studies p139
Unit review p80, **Finished?** p123			
Unit 7 **Keep calm!** p82	Feelings p83 Expressions with *heart* and *mind* p86	Gerunds and infinitives p85 Subject and object questions p87	A magazine interview: The power of 'not yet' p84 A report about schools in Denmark p90 Happiness around the world p90
Unit review p92, **Finished?** p124			
Unit 8 **Advertising** p94	Advertising p95 Internet verbs p98	Defining and non-defining relative clauses p97 Indefinite, reflexive and reciprocal pronouns p99	A report: Online advertising p96 Art and design: How to design an effective print advert p140
Unit review p104, **Finished?** p125			
Unit 9 **Have you heard the news?** p106	Reporting verbs p107 Adverbs of time and manner p110	Reported statements and commands p109 Reported questions p111	A newspaper story: International twins! p108 A story: Maori storytelling – How Maui slowed the Sun p114 Stories on stage p114
Unit review p116, **Finished?** p126			

Vocabulary Bank p132–136 **CLIL** p139–140 **Pronunciation** p142 **Irregular verbs** p143

Listening	Speaking and pronunciation	Writing	Project	Learn to Learn
A virtual reality tour p62	Expressing surprise and disbelief p64 The letters *mb* and *bt* p142	A competition entry p65		Learning verbs with prepositions p59 Listening for specific information p62 Skimming for gist p66 Learn to … use a presentation plan p69
A podcast p74	Encouraging a friend to do something p76 Stress in multi-syllable words p142	A for and against essay p77	The citizenship project: a leaflet p78 *How to* motivate yourself and your peers p78	Using collocations in sentences p71 Listening and choosing the correct option p74 Learn to … take responsibility for your learning p81
A conversation p86	Expressing sympathy and concern p88 Initial consonant clusters with *s* p142	An email reply p89		Remembering adjectives p83 Gapped flashcards p86 Synonyms and antonyms p91 Learn to … give your partner useful feedback p93
An interview p98	Recommending an online tool p100 The letters *-tion* p142	An online product review p101	The art and design project: an advert storyboard p102 *How to* give feedback p102	Wordbuilding: nouns and verbs p95 Open-ended questions p98 Learn to … work out the meaning of new words p105
A news report p110	Telling an anecdote p112 The letters *cia* p142	A news story p113		Telling stories to remember new words p107 Collaborative listening p110 Irregular adjective and noun pairs p115 Learn to … ask for help when you don't understand p117

5 WONDERFUL WORLD

LEARNING OUTCOMES

I can …

- understand texts about smart cities and a virtual reality tour
- express surprise and disbelief
- write a competition entry
- understand how to use the passive, question tags and questions with prepositions
- use verbs related to processes and extreme adjectives
- learn verbs with prepositions, listen for specific information and skim read to understand the general idea.

Start it!

1 Look at the photo of the Northern Lights. What does it look like?
2 Before you watch, can you think of any natural wonders?
3 What does a waterfall in Yosemite National Park look like? Watch and check.
4 Which is your favourite natural wonder? Why?

Watch video 5.1

p61

Language in action 5.2

p63

Language in action 5.3

p64

Everyday English 5.4

p66

Globetrotters 5.5

VOCABULARY

Processes

5.01 **1 Read about three amazing animals. Listen and repeat the words in bold.**

2 Match the words in bold in the text with definitions a–l.

a make something exist *create*
b make something come nearer ______
c get a new quality/ability ______
d take somewhere ______
e find the size ______
f join ______
g bring together ______
h make something ______
i give ______
j find the answer ______
k share information ______
l use too much ______

Bees **measure** distances between new flowers and their hive. They **communicate** this information by dancing for other bees, which then **collect** the nectar and **deliver** it to the hive. Nectar and pollen **supply** the nutrients bees need to live.

Spiders **create** webs to **attract** as well as catch insects. The silk they **produce** is five times as strong as steel, but they have to wait for the wind to **connect** the end of the first line to something nearby. Spiders don't **waste** any silk: they sometimes eat their webs when they have finished with them.

Crows **solve** problems to get food. In some cities they **develop** the ability to read traffic lights; they wait for the red light, place a walnut in the road, then fly up and wait for a car to drive over the nut and break it open.

LEARN TO LEARN

Learning verbs with prepositions

Learn verbs with the prepositions they take. This helps you to use them correctly.

3 Complete each sentence with a preposition (*to* or *with*). Sometimes both are possible.

1 Insects are **attracted** *to* spider webs.
2 Spiders **connect** their webs ______ something nearby.
3 Bees **communicate** ______ each other by dancing.
4 Bees collect nectar and **deliver** it ______ other bees.
5 Nectar **supplies** bees ______ nutrients.

4 Circle the correct words.

1 Which puzzle has six sides and is difficult to *solve* / *deliver*?
2 Which North American country *measures* / *supplies* length in inches and feet, not centimetres and metres?
3 Which country *produces* / *attracts* the most films every year?
4 What's the name of the tunnel that *wastes* / *connects* the UK with France?
5 How do dolphins *communicate* / *develop* with each other?
6 Which animals *create* / *collect* nuts for the winter?

Use it!

5 Discuss the questions in Exercise 4.

Explore it!

Guess the correct answer.

Bees beat their wings very fast, but how many times per second?

a 100 b 200 c 300

Find an interesting fact about birds or insects. Write a question for your partner to answer.

READING

A webzine article

5.02 **1 Look at the photo. What do you think a smart city is? Read the webzine article and find out.**

2 Match headings a–d with paragraphs 1–4.

a Soon to become a reality

b Greener streets

c Everything will be connected

d More choices for citizens

3 Read the webzine article again and discuss the questions.

1 How will the IOT make urban life better?

2 What will 3-D printers be able to do?

3 How will food be delivered to our homes?

4 How will we be healthier?

5 Why won't electricity be wasted?

6 What percentage of people will be living in rural areas by 2050?

4 Find words in the webzine article that mean:

1 the number of people living in a place (paragraph 1) ____________

2 belong or relating to the city (paragraph 1)

3 a small flying machine without a pilot (paragraph 2) ____________

4 to stop something happening (paragraph 3) ____________

5 the people who live in a particular place (paragraph 4) ____________

Voice it!

5 Discuss the questions.

1 What disadvantages might there be to living in a smart city? Think of three ideas.

2 Would you like to live in a smart city? Tell your partner and explain your reasons.

Finished? p122 Ex 1

SMART CITIES OF THE FUTURE

1 ☐ Electric cars, drone deliveries, houses that communicate with you when you're out. Are you attracted by this image of city life? If so, you're not alone. Scientists and engineers around the world are developing a huge digital web called the Internet of Things (IOT) that will make all of this possible. Soon, billions of devices will be connected by the IOT. It will collect all sorts of data – information about the weather, the traffic, population movement, our shopping, the places we visit, even our health. This information will be used to make urban life better for everyone. Welcome to smart cities, the cities of the future.

2 ☐ In smart cities, we'll have more free time. For example, imagine you're feeling hungry on the way home but don't want to cook. All you'll need to do is send a message to your 3-D printer and tell it to print something tasty for you. Or, if you prefer, order a takeaway and within minutes a delicious pizza is delivered by a drone. Smart citizens will be healthier too. Our fridges will remind us when it's time to buy fresh fruit and vegetables, while devices on our bodies will measure our levels of fitness. The data they collect will be supplied to our doctors and we'll be told to visit them as soon as anything is wrong, so we won't be surprised by unexpected health problems.

3 ☐ Smart cities will also be better for the environment, because electricity won't be wasted in them. Imagine you forget to turn the lights off when you go out. Don't worry – your house will do it for you. What's more, streetlights will only be switched on when you walk past them and cars will communicate with traffic lights to prevent traffic jams, saving both time and energy.

4 ☐ When the first cities were built thousands of years ago, their inhabitants couldn't have realised how different urban life would become, but smart cities are nearly here. Will everything and everyone soon be connected by the IOT? Probably not, but by 2050 more than 70% of us will be living in a city, and we'll definitely be even more connected than we are today.

LANGUAGE IN ACTION
The passive

Watch video 5.2
How did people listen to music in the past?
How will our clothes be made in the future?

Present	Past	Future
A pizza [1]_____ **delivered** by a drone.	The first cities [2]_____ **built** thousands of years ago.	Billions of devices [3]_____ **connected** by the IOT.
Time and energy **aren't wasted**.	Hieroglyphics **weren't understood** until 1822.	We [4]_____ **surprised** by unexpected health problems.
[5]_____ you **attracted** by this image of city life?	When **was** the Internet **invented**?	[6]_____ everything and everyone soon _____ **connected** by the IOT?

1 **Complete the examples in the table above. Use the webzine article on page 60 to help you.**

2 **Rewrite the sentences in the present or past with a passive form of the verb in bold and *by*.**

1 Moving objects **attract** bulls.
Bulls are attracted by moving objects.

2 Lightning **strikes** men more often than women.
_____

3 The Romans **didn't invent** Roman letters.
_____

4 Elizabeth Magie **invented** Monopoly.
_____

3 **Complete the text with the verbs in the box in the present and past passive.**

build	bury	lift	make
place	pull	use	~~visit~~

The Pyramids of Giza in Egypt [1] *are visited* by millions of tourists every year. When they [2]_____, about 5,500 years ago, great kings called pharaohs [3]_____ inside them. What we don't know is how the Pyramids [4]_____. More than two million blocks of stone [5]_____ for each one, but nobody knows how each stone [6]_____ in the correct position. Clearly, they [7]_____ by hand, because they were too heavy. [8]_____ they _____ by ropes or did people push them by hand?

5.03 **4** **Complete the conversation with the future passive of the verbs in brackets. Listen and check.**

A I was reading a blog that said in the future many jobs [1] *will be done* (do) by robots.

B Really? Like what?

A Well, food [2]_____ (serve) by them in restaurants, houses [3]_____ (build) by them – and in some schools, classes [4]_____ (teach) by them.

B Robot teachers! That will be strange. But [5]_____ all humans _____ (replace) by robots?

A I don't think so. The blog said most operations [6]_____ (not do) by robots – human doctors and surgeons will still do those.

B What about sports? [7]_____ human football players _____ (replace) completely?

A I don't think so, but who knows?

B I hope not, because that's what I want to be in the future!

Use it!

5 **Discuss the questions.**

1 Will all lessons be taught in English?

2 Will all shopping be done online?

Some lessons will be taught in English, but not all of them.

Finished? p122 Ex 2

LISTENING AND VOCABULARY

A virtual reality tour

1 Look at photos 1–3. Do you know where these places are?

5.04 **2** Listen to the virtual tour and check your answers to Exercise 1.

LEARN TO LEARN

Listening for specific information

Knowing what kind of information we are listening for can help us to hear it.

3 Read the sentences and decide if the missing information is a year, a measurement or a number.

1. There are seven New Wonders of the Natural World. a number
2. A major sports event took place in South Africa in ________. ________
3. The top of Table Mountain is ________ wide. ________
4. The biggest Komodo dragons are ________ long. ________
5. There are approximately ________ Komodo dragons on Komodo Island. ________
6. ________ smaller waterfalls make up Iguazu Falls. ________
7. The water falls up to ________. ________

5.04 **4** Listen again and complete the sentences in Exercise 3.

Extreme adjectives

5.05 **5** Replace the underlined words in the text with the words in the box. Listen and check.

boiling	deafening	dreadful	enormous	fascinating
freezing	gorgeous	marvellous	~~stunning~~	terrifying

The Sahara Desert looks [1]very beautiful stunning. I've been learning about it in class. It's [2]very interesting ________. At 9.2 million km^2, it's [3]very big ________. The sand dunes are [4]very beautiful ________. It would be [5]very good ________ to visit it one day, but it would be [6]very scary ________ to get lost there without water. During the day it's [7]very hot ________, but at night it can be [8]very cold ________. Sometimes there are sandstorms with [9]very loud ________ winds. It must be [10]very bad ________ to be caught in one.

Get it right!

We don't use *very* with extreme adjectives, but we can use ***really*** or ***absolutely***.

Use it!

6 Discuss the questions.

1. Where can you find stunning scenery in your country?
2. Which is worse, boiling hot or freezing cold weather? Why?
3. Would you prefer to live in a gorgeous, tiny house or an ugly, enormous house? Why?
4. What's the most fascinating school subject? Why?

There is an enormous waterfall in my country. The noise is deafening when you stand next to it.

Watch video 5.3
What is her vlog about?
What was she most impressed by?

LANGUAGE IN ACTION

Question tags and questions with prepositions

	Positive sentence + negative tag	Negative sentence + positive tag
to be	It**'s** Cape Town, **isn't** it?	It **isn't** Sydney, [1]______ it?
auxiliary *have*	The lesson **has** finished, [2]______ it?	Ivan **hasn't** arrived yet, **has** he?
modal verbs	The speech **will** be recorded, **won't** it?	You **won't** be eaten, [3]______ you?
present simple	You **speak** German, [4]______ you?	They **don't live** here, **do** they?
past simple	Linda **went** home early, **didn't** she?	You **didn't tell** anyone our secret, [5]______ you?

Question tags

1 **Complete the examples in the table above.**

2 **Complete the sentences with the correct question tag.**

1 That tour was very good, wasn't it?
2 Insects are interesting, ________?
3 It's not very hot in here, ________?
4 We can't hear each other, ________?
5 It would be scary to see a ghost, ________?

3 **Match the sentences in Exercise 1 with responses a–e. Complete the responses with the adjectives in the box.**

deafening fascinating freezing marvellous ~~terrifying~~

a Yes, it would be terrifying. [5]
b No, it's absolutely ________. [ ]
c No – the music is ________. [ ]
d It was ________. [ ]
e Yes, they're really ________. [ ]

Questions with prepositions

What are we learning [1]______ today?	Where are we going [2]______ next?
What are you looking [3]______?	What are you scared [4]______?
Who was it won [5]______?	Who do you look [6]______?

4 **Complete the examples in the table above with *about*, *at*, *by*, *like*, *of* or *to*.**

5 **Put the words in the correct order to make sentences. Then circle the correct answers.**

1 made / what / Tutankhamen's mask / of / was / ?
____
a glass b gold c silver

2 to / Apollo 11 / where / did / go / ?
____
a Mars b the moon c The International Space Station

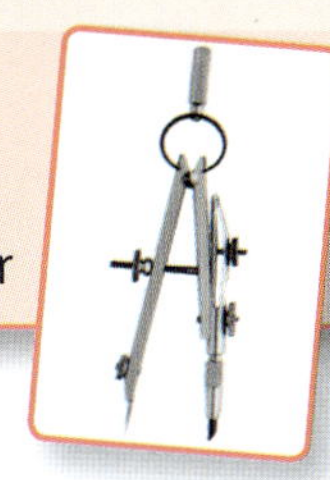

3 a compass / what / for / used / is / ?
____
a making holes b drawing circles c cutting paper

Use it!

6 **Discuss the questions using question tags.**

1 Who was *Don Quijote* written by?
2 What is a GPS used for?
3 What is glass made of?

Who was Don Quijote *written by?*

It was written by … , wasn't it?

Finished? p122 Ex 3

SPEAKING

Expressing surprise and disbelief

5.06 **1 What do you know about the building in the picture? Listen to the conversation. What do you learn about it?**

5.06 **2 Complete the conversation with the phrases from the *Useful language* box. Listen and check.**

ANGELA So, Ryan, how was your trip to Rome?
RYAN Oh, man, you should go. It's absolutely stunning. There's so much history and so many amazing buildings there. I loved it.
ANGELA Where was your favourite place?
RYAN I'd say it was the Coliseum.
ANGELA That's where the gladiators used to fight, isn't it?
RYAN Got it in one. Sometimes they would fight with animals, too. Bears, lions, elephants.
ANGELA You 1 *can't be serious*. With animals?
RYAN Yep. On one occasion over 10,000 animals were killed in a single day.
ANGELA 2 __________ me? That's dreadful!
RYAN And they used to have sea battles there.
ANGELA I find 3 __________. How was that done?
RYAN They would fill the stadium with water from the aqueducts. There were real ships and everything.
ANGELA: 4 __________? That's fascinating.
RYAN Wanna see a photo of me dressed as a gladiator outside?
ANGELA OK, go on. Wow! Is that you? I can't 5 __________ wore that!
RYAN I look terrifying, don't I?
ANGELA Er, not exactly. You look sweaty. It must've been really hot there.
RYAN It was. It was boiling.

Useful language

Are you kidding me?	Seriously?
I can't believe you actually …	You can't be serious.
I find that hard to believe.	

3 Complete the dialogues with the phrases in the *Everyday English* box.

1 A What's the best place you've ever been to?
B __________ Iceland.
2 A How was the movie?
B __________, I loved it!
3 A The exam was easy, wasn't it?
B __________. I think it was quite hard.
4 A Jack's house is enormous, isn't it?
B I know! It's got a pool __________.
5 A __________ have a picnic tomorrow?
B I can't, sorry. I'm busy.

Watch video 5.4
Everyday English

… and everything Er, not exactly. I'd say it was … Oh, man Wanna … ?

PLAN

4 Write about an amazing place you have been to. Think of three interesting things about it.

SPEAK

5 Practise the conversation. Describe your amazing place and ask your partner about their place. Remember to use the passive, question tags, questions with prepositions and phrases from the *Useful language* and *Everyday English* boxes.

CHECK

6 Work with another pair. Listen to their conversation and complete the notes.

What place did they talk about? __________

What was interesting about it? __________

Would you like to visit it? __________

WRITING
A competition entry

1 **Look at the photo. What do you think the building is? Read the competition entry and check your ideas.**

1 ☐ I've been to lots of amazing places, but the one that impressed me the most was Petra, an ancient city in Jordan. I visited it last summer with my family. We all loved it.

2 ☐ Petra is fascinating. The first buildings were built over 2,000 years ago. At one time it was inhabited by 30,000 people. A lot of it was carved out of the rock of the mountains. In fact, it is sometimes known as 'the Rose City' because of the colour of the rock.

3 ☐ The highlight of a visit to Petra is the Treasury. Nobody is sure why it was built, but archaeologists think that a king was buried there or that it was a place for important documents. When the sun shines on the front of the building, it's really stunning. I'm absolutely certain that it will still be visited hundreds of years in the future.

4 ☐ I think Petra deserves to win because it is so beautiful, especially the Treasury. Without a doubt, it's one of the most incredible places in the world.

GO GLOBAL
Tell us about the most incredible place you've ever visited to win two air tickets!

2 **Read the entry again. Match topics a–d with paragraphs 1–4.**

a The reason why the place should win
b Introduction
c Detailed description of part of the place
d General description of the place

3 **Discuss the questions.**

1 What is unusual about the way Petra was built?
2 What do people think the Treasury was built for?
3 List all the extreme adjectives in the entry.

4 **Match phrases 1–5 with the phrases from the *Useful language* box a–e with a similar meaning.**

1 for me, the … that was best was … ☐
2 It's certain that … ☐
3 I'm completely sure that … ☐
4 … should win because … ☐
5 When you go to …, the best part is … ☐

Useful language

a … deserves to win because …
b I'm absolutely certain that …
c The highlight of a visit to … is …
d the … that impressed me the most was …
e Without a doubt …

Write a competition entry.

PLAN

5 **Think of the most incredible place you have visited. Find out information about it and write down two reasons why it impressed you.**

WRITE

6 **Write your competition entry. Remember to include the four paragraphs in Exercise 2, extreme adjectives and phrases from the *Useful language* box.**

CHECK

7 **Do you …**

- give a description of the place?
- say why it impressed you?
- explain why you think the place should win?

Pronunciation p142
Finished? p122 Ex 4

AROUND THE WORLD

READING
A travel blog

Globetrotters

Watch video 5.5
Extreme homes

- What can make a place difficult to live in?
- Why is it difficult to live in these places: Atacama Desert, Siberia and Lake Titicaca?
- What's unusual about Matera?

1 **Look at the pictures. Where do you think they were taken?**

5.09 2 **Read Scott's blog for Day 1. Which activities that you can do in Meghalaya does he mention?**

LEARN TO LEARN
Skimming for gist

Often you want to understand the general idea of a text, not the details. To do this you can 'skim' the text, which means to read it very quickly.

3 **Skim the rest of the blog. Which of the activities that Scott mentions in Day 1 of his blog does he not do while he is in Meghalaya?**

SCOTT THE EXPLORER
BLOGGING MY WAY AROUND INDIA

DAY 1
Hi, everyone! This week I'm in Meghalaya in northeast India, the wettest place on Earth. I've only been here for a day but I love the place already. It's really cloudy, but when the clouds lift the scenery is stunning: beautiful mountains covered by gorgeous green forests. The people are really friendly, and there are loads of things to do – you can go to festivals, explore caves, see waterfalls, visit a bird sanctuary, cross 'living root bridges', go trekking and so much more. I can't wait! This blog will be updated while I'm here so make sure you check out my posts!

DAY 2
This morning I went to the marvellous Siju Bird Sanctuary, where lots of endangered birds are protected. I even saw one of the rare peacock pheasants. Check out the photo! After that I tried *jadoh*, a local dish of rice and meat. Rice is traditionally eaten several times a day here, and it was delicious. In the afternoon I wanted to explore the capital, Shillong, where I'm staying, but it started raining heavily, so I stayed inside and relaxed. Tomorrow I'm going to visit the Krem Lymput cave. I'm really excited – I've never been in a cave before!

DAY 3

OK, I've just got back from the cave tour. It wasn't my favourite experience! The guide was great. He explained everything really clearly – how old the cave is, how it was made and so on, and the cave was beautiful, but at times I was really scared. It's over six km long, with some enormous rooms, but most of it was narrow, dark and wet. I had to carry a torch and walk really carefully. It was terrifying! Anyway, I'm safely back in the hostel now. More from me tomorrow!

DAY 4

Today I saw the Nongkrem dance festival. This colourful festival is celebrated by the Khasi people, who are one of the main groups of people in Meghalaya. They have an incredibly fascinating society. Women have a very important role in Meghalaya society. For example, the birth of a boy is not a special occasion but the birth of a girl is celebrated by everyone, children take their mother's surname, and when parents die, the youngest daughter gets their house. It's not the best place to be a boy. The sons don't really get anything!

DAY 5

DAY 6

I'm back! I didn't write anything yesterday because I was trekking in the mountains overnight. I saw some incredible views and finally crossed one of the famous tree root bridges. These bridges are created by hand. People tie the roots of young trees together and help them to grow slowly across rivers. The process takes many years, but eventually the roots are strong enough for people to walk on. Check out the picture I took! Anyway, the time here has gone so fast. I'd love to stay longer but tomorrow I have to leave. Thanks for reading!

4 (5.10) **Now read the whole of Scott's blog. Discuss the questions.**

1. What problem did Scott have on Day 2?
2. Do you think Scott will visit any more caves in the future? Why / Why not?
3. What is unusual about births in Khasi society?
4. Why didn't Scott post anything on Day 5?
5. How are 'living root bridges' made?

5 Find adverbs in the travel blog that mean:

1. in a traditional way (day 2) ______
2. a lot (day 2) ______
3. in a way that is easy to understand (day 3) ______
4. absolutely (day 4) ______
5. in the end (day 6) ______

Voice it!

6 Discuss the questions.

1. Would you like to visit Meghalaya? Why / Why not?
2. Are boys and girls treated the same in your country?

Explore it!

Guess the correct answer.

Meghalaya is the wettest place on Earth, but where is the driest?

a in South America
b in Africa c in Australia

Find another interesting fact about an extreme place on Earth. Write a question for your partner to answer.

OWN IT! The Culture Project Teacher's Resource Bank

5 REVIEW

VOCABULARY

1 Complete the sentences with the correct form of the verbs in the box.

attract collect communicate connect create deliver develop measure produce solve supply waste

1 The postman ___________ seven letters to my house this morning.
2 The teacher ___________ the students' homework next Monday.
3 Scientists ___________ the Internet in the 1970s.
4 Most people ___________ lots of plastic every day.
5 My car engine ___________ a lot of heat.
6 Electric lights ___________ different insects.
7 Walt Disney ___________ some of the world's most famous cartoon characters.
8 A stopwatch ___________ time.
9 A young mathematician ___________ the most difficult equation in history a few years ago.
10 Three different companies ___________ electricity to this city next year.
11 The Channel Tunnel ___________ the United Kingdom with France.
12 Pilots on international flights use English ___________ with each other.

2 Complete the sentences with the adjectives in the box.

boiling deafening dreadful enormous fascinating freezing terrifying

1 Turn that music down – it's ___________!
2 Can you open the window? It's ___________ in here.
3 It was a bad movie – the actors were ___________.
4 The Grand Canyon? is 446 km long – it's ___________.
5 Put your coat on. It's ___________ today.
6 I'm scared of spiders. They're ___________.
7 The book was ___________. I read it twice!

LANGUAGE IN ACTION

3 Rewrite sentences 1 to 5 in Exercise 1 as passive sentences.

1 ___________
2 ___________
3 ___________
4 ___________
5 ___________

4 Complete the dialogue with the correct questions and question tags.

A looking / you / what / for / are
[1] ___________?
B My phone charger. It was here somewhere.
A You haven't put it in your bag, [2] ___________?
B No, I looked there. You don't have an extra one, [3] ___________?
A Sorry, no. to / you / who / do / to / talk / need
[4] ___________?
B My brother. We're going to a rugby match. It starts in 15 minutes.
A He can just wait for you inside the stadium, [5] ___________?
B: No, because I've got the tickets!

Self-assessment

I can use verbs to talk about processes.

I can use extreme adjectives.

I can use the passive.

I can use question tags and questions with prepositions.

LEARN TO ... USE A PRESENTATION PLAN

A presentation plan can help you prepare a presentation and make it clear and easy for the listener to understand.

1 Read Kirill's presentation plan notes. What do you think his presentation is about? Circle a, b or c.

a a rainbow

b a total eclipse of the sun

c the aurora borealis

Presentation Plan

Question		Notes
Introduce the presentation.		Today, I'm going to talk about …
1 *What is it?*		a very special event in the sky!
2 *How does it happen?*		the sun is hidden by the moon, parts of the Earth are covered by its shadow
3 *Where and when can you see it?*	**Where?**	You need to be in the area covered by the moon's shadow.
	When?	about once every year and a half
4 *What other information can I give you?*		Never look directly at it! It's dangerous.
5 *Have I ever seen one?*	**Where?**	Yes, in Russia
	When?	11 August, 2018
	What was it like?	absolutely stunning!

2 Read the beginning of Kirill's presentation. Complete the missing questions.

Good afternoon. Today, I'm going to talk about a total eclipse of the sun. Perhaps you've seen one. [1] What is it? *Well, it's a very special event in the sky.* [2] ______ *It happens when the sun is hidden by the moon and parts of the Earth are covered by its shadow.* [3] ______ *Well, you can only see it …*

3 Imagine you are doing Kirill's presentation together. Use the questions and the notes to do the complete presentation.

OWN IT!

4 Prepare a presentation on how a rainbow is formed. Use the information below to help you.

How is a rainbow formed?

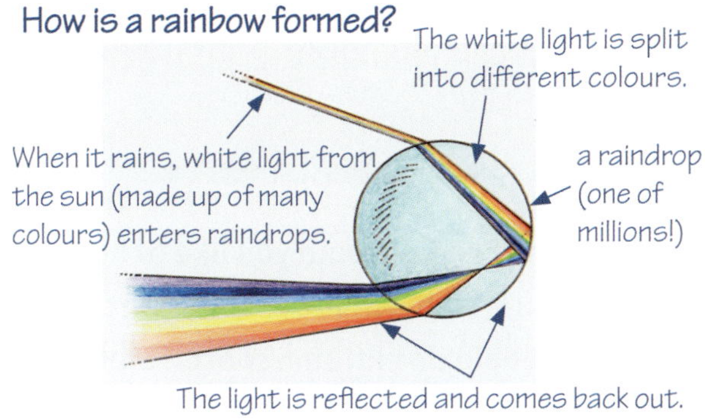

- We see the coloured light from all the millions of raindrops as a rainbow.
- You can see rainbows in the sky opposite the sun.
- Rainbows are really circles, but we only see half.
- If you're lucky, you might see a double rainbow

5 Listen to your partner's presentation and ask a question.

6 NO LIMITS

LEARNING OUTCOMES

I can ...

- understand texts about taking risks and overcoming challenges
- encourage a friend to do something
- write a for and against essay
- understand how to use conditional tenses
- use verb collocations with *get*, *take* and *have*, and talk about inspirations and challenges
- use collocations in sentences, and practise listen and choose questions
- make a leaflet.

Start it!

1 Look at the photo. Would you like to do a sport like this?
2 Before you watch, what extreme sports can you think of?
3 Why do people do extreme sports? Watch and check.
4 Are there any extreme sports you'd like to do? Which ones?

Watch video 6.1

p73

Language in action 6.2

p75

Language in action 6.3

p76

Everyday English 6.4

VOCABULARY
Verb collocations with *get*, *take* and *have*

6.01 **1** **Read the quiz. Match the phrases in bold with definitions a–l. Listen and repeat the phrases.**

a annoy somebody a lot *get on my nerves*
b become unhappy because something is not interesting ______
c do something that might be dangerous ______
d enjoy yourself ______
e be interested in something ______
f feel unsure about something ______
g get enjoyment from something ______
h have the possibility to do something ______
i not know where you are ______
j get a good feeling from something ______
k spend time with somebody so you learn more about them ______
l use the good things from a situation ______

1
A I **get bored** when I watch a film I've seen before.
B I **take pleasure in** watching films a second or third time.

2
A I like **taking advantage of** being in unknown places by myself to explore.
B I never walk around new places by myself in case I **get lost**.

3
A I **get a lot out of** extreme sports like skiing or waterskiing.
B I don't like to **take risks** and would never do extreme sports.

4
A I try new foods whenever I **have the chance**.
B I **have doubts** about trying new foods I've never eaten before.

5
A I like **getting to know** people who are exciting and unpredictable.
B People who are unpredictable sometimes **get on my nerves**.

6
A I **take an interest in** all kinds of fun activities, like going on theme park rides.
B I don't **have fun** on theme park rides. They scare me!

Did you choose more As or more Bs?
More As – You enjoy taking risks and like to experience new, exciting situations.
More Bs – You prefer not to take lots of risks and enjoy being in a routine.

Pronunciation p142

2 **Read the quiz again. Circle the answers that are true for you.**

3 **Read the results at the bottom of the page. Do you agree with them?**

LEARN TO LEARN
Using collocations in sentences

Collocations with *get*, *take* and *have* have lots of meanings. Record these collocations in a sentence to remember the meaning.

4 **Think of true sentences for the collocations in Exercise 1. Use *always*, *usually*, *sometimes*, *hardly ever*, *never*.**

I sometimes get bored when I'm at home.

5 **Compare your sentences with your partner. What other collocations do you know with *get*, *have* and *take*?**

Use it!

6 **Write questions with the collocations. Ask and answer the questions.**

______
______
______
______
______

Have you ever had the chance to try an extreme sport?

Yes, I had the chance to try waterskiing last summer. I had lots of fun!

Explore it!

Guess the correct answer.

How old was the oldest person to skydive?

a 89 **b** 102 **c** 110

Find another fact about an extreme sport. Write a question for your partner to answer.

When taking risks is a *good thing*

Everyone has to take risks sometimes, but many people think risks are negative, especially for teenagers. They connect risk-taking with dangerous behaviour, such as riding a motorbike too fast or looking at your phone while crossing the street. If this sounds like your parents, you might want to explain this to them. Taking risks can also be positive. Sometimes feeling scared or uncomfortable can help us experience new things and learn how to make good decisions. If more people understood this, they might see why teenagers sometimes need to take risks.

What type of risks do you like?

Surprises Would you be happy if your friends planned a surprise party for you? If the answer is yes, then you may enjoy unpredictable things. You get bored very easily and take pleasure in not knowing what's going to happen next.

Danger If you take an interest in activities such as skiing or parkour, you might enjoy danger. If you adore extreme sports or theme park rides, it's because risky situations produce a chemical in the brain called dopamine. Dopamine makes you feel happy and want to repeat an activity again to get the same feeling. That's why you want to go back on a rollercoaster ride as soon as it's finished.

New experiences Alternatively, if you have fun trying new foods or discovering new places, you may be someone who gets a lot out of new experiences. This is important because if you didn't go to new places, you wouldn't learn new things about other cultures.

Healthy risks

How would you feel if you had an audition for the school show? Auditions, selection to get into a school sports team or facing a school bully are situations that might make you feel scared. However, they also help you develop important skills such as how to solve problems, make good decisions and become independent. Just think, you could be the world's best singer, lawyer or volleyball player. But unless you take some risks, you'll never know.

READING

A fact sheet

1 (6.04) **How do the people in the photos feel? How would you feel? Read the fact sheet and check your ideas.**

2 Read the fact sheet again and complete the table.

Types of risk taker	1 People who like *unpredictable things* . 2 People who like ______ . 3 People who like ______ .
Examples of negative risks	
Examples of positive risks	
Skills you develop when you take risks	

3 Read the fact sheet again. Write *T* (true), *F* (false) or *DS* (doesn't say).

1. All risks are dangerous. *F*
2. Most parents don't want teenagers to take risks. ___
3. Some people like not knowing what will happen. ___
4. You have more dopamine in your brain when you feel bored. ___
5. Taking risks can teach us about other cultures. ___
6. There are advantages to scary situations. ___
7. If you don't take risks, you won't solve problems. ___

4 Find words in the fact sheet that mean:

1. something that can change suddenly (adj) ______
2. love (v) ______
3. if something bad could happen (adj) ______
4. another possibility (adv) ______
5. choosing someone from a group of people (n) ______

Voice it!

5 Discuss the questions.

1. What type of risk taker is most similar to you? Why?
2. What risky things have you done that aren't dangerous, e.g. having an audition?
3. Can taking risks help solve problems?

Finished? p123 Ex 1

LANGUAGE IN ACTION

First and second conditional

Watch video 6.2
What did he try last week?
Did he like it?

First conditional	Second conditional
If this [1]________ (sound) like your parents, you **might want** to explain this to them.	If you **took** healthy risks, you **could become** more independent.
Unless you [2]________ (take) some risks, you**'ll** never **know**.	**If** you [3]________ (not go) to new places, you **wouldn't learn** new things about other cultures.
Will you **go** on all the rides **if** we **go** to the theme park?	**Would** you **be** happy if your friends [4]________ (plan) a surprise party for you?

1 **Complete the examples in the table above with the correct form of the verbs in brackets. Use the fact sheet on page 72 to help you.**

Get it right!

We can use ***unless*** to mean *except if*.
Use a positive verb with *unless*.

I'll go to the beach unless it rains = I'll go to the beach except if it rains.

2 **Put the words in the correct order to make first conditional sentences.**

1 you'll / get better at it / If you / a lot, / practise parkour
If you practise parkour a lot, you'll get better at it.

2 from other cultures / if you / You might / try it / enjoy food
____

3 will you / doesn't rain / go to / If it / the water park / ?
____

3 **Complete the second conditional sentences with the correct form of the verbs.**

1 Would you learn to fly a plane if you had the chance? (would / have / learn)

2 If we ________ crazy things from time to time, life ________ boring. (could / be / not do)

3 I ________ frightened if I ________ in a forest at night. (wouldn't / get lost / be)

4 **Complete the text with the first or second conditional.**

If you [1]had (have) the chance, would you risk your life to save someone? If you thought about it carefully, you probably [2]________ (not put) yourself in danger, but scientists say it's a natural impulse. For example, if we [3]________ (see) someone in the water who couldn't swim, we would save them. In an emergency, unless we [4]________ (stop) and [5]________ (think) about it, the human body will react automatically.

Use it!

5 **Make questions with *you* in the first or second conditional. Ask and answer.**

1 If / not meet / friends / later / might / feel?
If you don't meet your friends later, how might you feel?

2 How / life / different / not have / social media?
____

3 What / do this weekend / have some free time?
____

4 Which extreme sport / try / could choose?
____

Finished? p123 Ex 2

VOCABULARY AND LISTENING

Inspiration and challenge

1 6.05 **Read the nomination for an amazing athlete. Match the words in bold with definitions a–j.**

Send us your nominations for the most amazing athlete you know and we'll tell their story on our podcast.

- Which athlete [1]**inspires** you because they have [2]**overcome** an [3]**obstacle**?
- Did they show [4]**determination** and [5]**bravery**? How?
- How did friends or family [6]**support** and [7]**encourage** them to get on with their life?
- What was their biggest [8]**challenge**?
- What have they [9]**achieved**?
- Have they had any [10]**opportunities** to help other people?

a deal with a difficult situation successfully ☐
b finish something or reach an aim after a lot of hard work ☐
c give confidence to others and motivate them to do something ☐
d give emotional or practical help to others ☐
e make someone feel they want to do something and can do it [1]
f no fear of dangerous or difficult things
g situations or chances ☐
h something which requires a lot of hard work to be done (successfully) ☐
i the ability to continue trying to do something difficult ☐
j something that stops an action or makes progress difficult or slow ☐

Use it!

2 **Discuss the questions.**

1 Who or what inspires you?
2 What's the biggest obstacle you or someone you know has overcome?
3 Who encourages you to do your homework?

A podcast

3 6.06 **Listen to the podcast. What big challenge did Bethany Hamilton overcome?**

LEARN TO LEARN

Listening and choosing the correct option

Read all the options, check any unknown words and cross out any options you know are not correct.

4 6.06 **Listen and circle the correct option.**

1 When she was 13 Bethany …
a learned to surf. b had an accident.
c gave up surfing.

- Check you understand *gave up* (past simple of *give up* – to stop something forever.)
- Option a isn't correct as she learned to surf when she was a young child.
- Option c isn't correct as she returned to surfing soon after the accident.
- The correct answer is option b.

5 6.07 **Listen to the whole extract and circle the correct options.**

2 Bethany lost her arm ….
a in the sea b in hospital
c three weeks after the accident

3 It was … decision to return to surfing.
a Bethany's b her family's c a bad

4 Bethany competes ….
a in special competitions
b only in the USA
c against other professional surfers

5 Her book and films ….
a are not true b teach people how to surf
c inspire people to overcome challenges

Voice it!

6 **What surprises you most about her story? What would you do in a similar situation?**

LANGUAGE IN ACTION
Third conditional

Watch video 6.3
What is she thinking about?
Where would she have gone on holiday?

[1] ________ situation in the past	[2] ________ consequence
If + **had** (**not**) + **past participle**	**would** (**not**) **have** + **past participle**
If they **hadn't taken** Bethany to hospital straight away, **If** that **had happened** to me,	she **would have died**. I **wouldn't have returned** to the water.
Question	
What **would** you **have done**	**if** it **had happened** to you?

1 **Complete the headings with *Possible* or *Imaginary*.**

2 **Put the words in the correct order to make third conditional sentences.**

1 had seen / she wouldn't / in the water / If Bethany / the shark / have gone

____

2 Many people wouldn't / if she / a film / have heard / hadn't made / about her bravery

____

6.08 **3** **Complete the third conditional sentences about stories 1–3. Use the verbs in brackets. Listen and check.**

1 A girl got stuck under a car and a high school baseball team lifted the car off the girl.

a If the girl hadn't got stuck (not get stuck), the team wouldn't have needed (not need) to lift the car.

b If the team ________ (not lift) the car, the girl ________ (not survive)

2 A 14-year-old saw a fire in his neighbour's home and went to help and saved a boy.

a If he ________ (not see) the fire, he ________ (not go) to help.

b If he ________ (not go) to help, he ________ (not save) the boy.

3 A group of teens were attacked by a bear in Alaska. One girl did first aid for nine hours until help arrived.

a If they ________ (not go) to Alaska, they ________ (not be) attacked.

b If help ________ (arrive) earlier, the girl ________ (not do) first aid for nine hours.

4 **Write a third conditional sentence for each situation.**

1 Alfie broke his leg when he went rock climbing.

If Alfie hadn't gone rock climbing, he wouldn't have broken his leg.

2 Four students got up late and missed the coach to France.

____

3 The school cook didn't make enough food and the students were hungry.

____

4 Class 4B went to Madrid and learned how to speak Spanish.

____

Use it!

5 **Complete the sentences about you.**

1 If I had been born in a different country ______________________________.

2 If I hadn't gone to this school ______________________________.

3 If I hadn't met my best friend ______________________________.

Finished? p123 Ex 3

SPEAKING
Encouraging a friend to do something

6.09 **1 Listen to Mia and Jack's conversation. Which activities do they discuss?**

6.09 **2 Complete the conversation with the phrases from the *Useful language* box. Listen and check.**

MIA Are you going to come whitewater rafting this weekend?
JACK I'm not sure. It looks a little scary to me.
MIA Oh, it's not really. I had so much fun when I went. [1] You'll never know unless you try, will you?
JACK But the water is so fast! It looks seriously deep and I'm not the world's best swimmer.
MIA Relax and [2] ____________. The instructors will look after you. They don't take any risks.
JACK Mmm, I'm still not sure.
MIA: Well what about paddle boarding? That's less risky.
JACK You've got to be joking! I wouldn't dare stand up on the board in the middle of the sea. [3] ____________ I fell in?
MIA Come on! It's easy! [4] ____________! If you fall in, you just get back on the board.
JACK [5] ____________, but I'm not like you. Water sports are a real challenge for me.
MIA Well, what if I practised with you?
JACK Hmm. That might help. OK, I'll come.
MIA Good for you! I promise [6] ____________ and you might even have fun! Let's go on Sunday.

Useful language

Encouraging
Don't worry, you'll be fine. You can do it!
You'll feel really proud afterwards.
You'll never know unless you try …

Responding
That's easy for you to say … What if … (+ past simple)?

Watch video 6.4
Everyday English

Come on! Good for you! not really
seriously You've got to be joking!

3 Match the phrases in the *Everyday English* box with their meanings 1–5.

1 extremely ________
2 not very ________
3 That's great! ________
4 to encourage someone to do something ________
5 You're not serious! ________

4 How do you say these phrases in your language?

PLAN

5 Make notes about something you want to encourage your partner to do. Use the ideas below or your own ideas.

do an audition for a school show
try an extreme sport

SPEAK

6 Practise trying to encourage your partner. Remember to use first, second and third conditionals, vocabulary from this unit and phrases from the *Useful language* and *Everyday English* boxes.

CHECK

7 Work with another pair. Listen to their conversation and complete the notes.

What did the other students encourage each other to do? ____________

Would you try the things in their conversation?
____

WRITING

A for and against essay

1 Think about a time when something went wrong for you. How did you feel? What did you learn?

2 Read the for and against essay. Circle the best title.

a Is it always bad when things go wrong?

b Should we try more new things?

1 There are times when things go wrong. For example, you might lose a sports match or fail an important exam. However, is it always negative when this happens?

2 On the one hand, when things go wrong we feel bad. For instance, if we fail a French exam, we might have doubts about our ability to speak the language and lose confidence. Furthermore, we might think we haven't got the skills to achieve our goals.

3 On the other hand, when we overcome a difficult situation we feel good. If we think about what went wrong, we might solve the problem in the future, such as by preparing for our next exam in a different way.

4 In conclusion, although it can feel negative when things go wrong, I personally believe that this is not always bad if we can learn something new. When we look for an opportunity to overcome the problem, we'll soon feel good again.

3 Read the essay again and discuss the questions.

1 How does the writer end the introduction? Why?

2 In which paragraph does the writer give their opinion?

3 Which paragraph talks about the negatives?

4 Which paragraph talks about the positives?

4 Complete the *Useful language* box with the phrases from the essay.

Useful language

introducing a new idea: Furthermore …, [1] ________

introducing the opposite idea: [2] ________

giving an example: For example …, [3] ________, [4] ________

giving an opinion: [5] ________

introducing a conclusion: [6] ________

Write your own for and against essay.

PLAN

5 Look at the essay title and make notes on your ideas and examples. Decide what information to include in each paragraph. Use the information in Exercise 3 to help you.

Should we take risks?

WRITE

6 Write your for and against essay. Remember to include four paragraphs, conditional tenses, vocabulary from this unit and phrases from the *Useful language* box.

CHECK

7 Do you …

- include an introduction?
- talk about the negatives?
- talk about the positives?
- have a conclusion?

Finished? p123 Ex 4

THE CITIZENSHIP PROJECT

A leaflet

1 **Look at the leaflet. Which two things does it aim to do?**

a inform b warn c entertain d persuade

6.10 2 **Read the leaflet and answer the questions.**

1 Who are the courses for?
2 Which activities can you do on each course?
3 On which course will you work in a team?
4 The courses are 'unplugged'. What does that mean?
5 Why might it be good to try one of the courses?

3 **Read the leaflet again and find these features.**

1 Title
2 Introduction to get readers interested
3 Details about the activities
4 Phrases to persuade people to do the course

How to motivate yourself and your peers

4 **Match 1–4 with a–d to make tips about how to motivate yourself and your peers on a project.**

1 Be clear about what you have to do.	a All projects have problems. Find a way to solve them.
2 Don't give up when there's an obstacle.	b Divide up the work equally.
3 Each person has a role.	c Have confidence in yourself and your team.
4 Believe you can do the project.	d If you don't understand something, ask.

6.11 5 **Listen to students working in a team at the start of their project. Put tips 1–4 in Exercise 4 in the order you hear them.**

___, ___, ___, ___

ON COURSE TO CONFIDENCE!

Are you 14–18? Do you get bored in the holidays? Do you like making friends, having fun and doing lots of exciting activities? If this sounds like you, then check out our courses and choose the one for you.

OUTDOOR SURVIVAL SKILLS

If you enjoy adventure and being outside in the fresh air, you will love this course. It's a great way to meet new people as you will be working in teams on different activities such as orienteering, building a fire and cooking outdoors. Some of the activities are challenging and you will have to work together and support each other to complete them.

WATER SPORTS

If your idea of fun is spending all day in the water, you will get a lot out of this course. You will have the chance to try everything from surfing and paddle boarding to scuba diving and whitewater rafting. If you've never tried water sports before, why not give them a go? You might be surprised at how much fun you have.

CLIMBING HIGH

One of our most popular courses is this confidence-building one. You will have the chance to go rock climbing and then abseil down again. You'll also go on a tree-top ropes course. If you'd like to learn a different skill, you could spend a day trying parkour.

Remember! All of our courses are unplugged, so leave your mobiles and other electronic devices at home. From day one you will discover that you don't have to be online to have fun.

We encourage you to take risks and try new things, so if you have never tried any of these sports, one of our courses is the perfect opportunity. Just think how good you'll feel if you overcome the fear to do something you've never done before!

PLAN

6 Work in groups. Make a list of courses for teenagers to build their confidence. Then choose two or three ideas and design a leaflet to inform and persuade people to do them. Complete the steps below.

- Draw a plan of the leaflet.
- Decide who prepares each section.
- Prepare your section with the features in Exercise 3.
- Show your section to someone else to check.
- Listen to your classmate's ideas and improve your section.
- Work together to make your leaflet.

PRESENT

7 Present your leaflet to your classmates. Remember to include information about the courses, the features in Exercise 3 and the tips in *How to* motivate yourself and your peers.

CHECK

8 Read your classmates' leaflets. Decide which activities you would like to do from their leaflets.

6 REVIEW

VOCABULARY

1 Circle the words which <u>don't</u> go with each verb.

1 get — *a lot out of something / risks / lost*
2 take — *pleasure in something / advantage of something / doubts*
3 have — *on someone's nerves / the chance to do something / fun*
4 get — *bored / to know someone / an interest in something*

2 Complete the sentences with the correct form of the words and phrases that don't go with the verbs in Exercise 1.

1 I had ____________ before I went rafting because I'm not a strong swimmer.
2 It can be positive to take ____________ because we learn to make decisions.
3 My brother has started to take ____________ photography.
4 My sister really gets ____________ . She's always taking my things.

3 Complete the sentences with the words in the box.

achieved	bravery	determination
opportunity	overcome	supported

1 She was awarded a prize for her ____________ in the fire.
2 My cousin finally ____________ his ambition to learn how to windsurf.
3 Do students have the ____________ to go to music classes at your school?
4 My parents ____________ my decision to do a bungee jump for charity.
5 He passed his final exams after a lot of hard work and ____________ .
6 Since I started swimming I have ____________ my fear of deep water.

LANGUAGE IN ACTION

4 Complete the sentences about parkour with the first or second conditional.

1 How quickly ____________ I ____________ (learn) if I practised every day?
2 If you already ____________ (do) regular sport or exercise, you may find it easy to learn.
3 If I ____________ (watch) parkour videos online, will I learn some techniques?
4 If you ____________ (train) every day for a month, you could learn to jump over walls.

5 Join the two sentences to make one sentence in the third conditional.

1 Mozart learned music as a young child. He wrote his first symphony when he was eight or nine.
____
____

2 Emma Watson studied drama as a child. She was Hermione in the Harry Potter films.
____
____

3 The artist van Gogh moved to Paris. Van Gogh met his friend Paul Gauguin in Paris.
____
____

4 J.R.R. Tolkien wrote *The Lord of the Rings*. Peter Jackson made a film trilogy of the book.
____
____

Self-assessment

I can use collocations with *get*, *take* and *have*.
I can use nouns and verbs for inspiration and challenge.
I can use the first and second conditional.
I can use the third conditional.

LEARN TO LEARN

LEARN TO ... TAKE RESPONSIBILITY FOR YOUR LEARNING

It's important to take responsibility for your own learning. This will help you to learn when you are outside your class as well.

1 Do the quiz and find out your score. Do you agree with what it says about you? Discuss the results with a partner.

Are you taking responsibility for your learning?

	Always	Sometimes	Never
1 When you're in class, how often do you ...			
a pay attention to the teacher's corrections?			
b try to help your partner speak and write better?			
c use spidergrams and presentation plans?			
2 When you want to learn new vocabulary, how often do you ...			
a write example sentences?			
b make and use flashcards?			
c use a monolingual (only English) dictionary?			
3 Outside class, how often do you ...			
a speak in English to other people?			
b watch TV series or films in English?			
c read books or articles in English online?			
4 Thinking about technology, how often do you ...			
a have English as the language on your phone and your apps?			
b use vocabulary learning apps?			
c listen to podcasts in English?			

5 

If you were travelling in an English-speaking country, would you ...	Always	Sometimes	Never
a speak English in shops and restaurants?			
b try to understand signs in English?			
c ask for directions in English if you got lost?			

Extra challenges!

- Write text messages to your friends in English.
- Send and receive voice messages with friends in English.
- Listen to music in English and look up the lyrics online.
- Read a 'graded reader' – a famous book made easier for learners.

Points: always = 2, sometimes = 1, never = 0.

0–3 points: You aren't taking much responsibility for your learning yet, but if you try more ideas from the quiz, you'll soon become a better learner!

4–7 points: You're taking some responsibility for your learning, but there's a lot more you could do if you tried. Take advantage of what you've learned in this quiz to think about how to improve.

8–10 points: You're taking lots of responsibility for your learning. That's great! Time for something new – try our extra challenges!

2 Look at the extra challenges. Which is the best idea? Write one more.

OWN IT!

3 Think about how to take more responsibility for your learning. Choose three ideas and tell your partner what you have chosen and why.

I've chosen 'read a graded reader' because I love books. If I'd known about them before, I'd have started one already!

7 KEEP CALM!

LEARNING OUTCOMES

I can …

- understand texts about a growth mindset and reducing exam stress
- express sympathy and concern
- write an email reply
- understand gerunds and infinitives, and subject and object questions
- use adjectives that describe feelings and expressions with *heart* and *mind*
- personalise vocabulary, make gapped flashcards, and learn synonyms and antonyms.

Start it!

1 Look at the photo. How is the girl feeling?
2 Before you watch, do you associate an emotion with these colours: red, grey, purple, yellow?
3 What colour can make you feel hungry? Watch and check.
4 What colours do you wear when you're happy and when you're sad?

Watch video 7.1

p85

Language in action 7.2

p87

Language in action 7.3

p88

Everyday English 7.4

p90

Globetrotters 7.5

VOCABULARY

Feelings

1 **Read the leaflet. Do you agree with it?**

7.01 2 **Match the words in bold in the leaflet with definitions 1–13. Listen, check and repeat.**

1 happy m
2 angry
3 unhappy
4 very silly
5 feeling thanks
6 not confident
7 enthusiastic
8 quiet and calm
9 in emotional pain
10 extremely happy
11 finding something funny
12 positive about the future
13 pleased to achieve something

7.02 3 **Listen and complete the sentences with one word.**

1 Sally feels absolutely ______.
2 The boy feels ______.
3 Mark felt absolutely ______.
4 The girl feels really ______.
5 Monica is feeling a bit ______.

LEARN TO LEARN

Remembering adjectives

Think about your personal experiences to help you remember new adjectives.

4 **Do Part 1 in the Stay happy! leaflet. Think of a sentence for each adjective.**

I feel amused when I watch comedy films.

5 **Say your sentences. Do you have similar or different ideas?**

I feel satisfied when I score a goal in football.

Use it!

6 **Now do Part 2 of the leaflet. Tell your partner your plans.**

STAY HAPPY!

For teenagers, life can be an emotional rollercoaster. Sometimes you're [a]**thrilled** to be alive, then you feel [b]**down** for no reason. You often feel [c]**insecure** about who you are, and [d]**annoyed** with every adult on the planet. You feel [e]**ridiculous** when you don't know something all your friends seem to know, and [f]**hurt** that nobody seems to care about what you're feeling. Of course, people do care, which is why we've created this exercise for developing positive emotions.

Part 1 For each word below (amused, etc.), think of a situation that helps you feel that emotion.

Part 2 Choose two positive emotions you want to practise. Do something which will increase those emotions every day for a week.

I feel …	This week I will …
[g]amused when my best friend tells me jokes.	ask him to tell me some every day.
[h]**hopeful** when I make a wish.	make three wishes about …
[i]**peaceful** when I walk on the beach.	
[j]**grateful** when people help me.	
[k]**eager** when I start a new art project.	
[l]**satisfied** when I've tidied my room.	
[m]**glad** when my friends are happy.	

Explore it!

Guess the correct answer.

Complete the expression *Laughter is the best …*

a communication. b exercise. c medicine.

Find out a fact about smiling. Write a question for your partner to answer.

READING

A magazine interview

1 **Read and answer the question at the beginning of the interview.**

7.03 **2** **Read the interview and match the interviewer's questions a–d with 1–4. Listen and check.**

a You had a fixed mindset?

b Malcolm, what exactly is a growth mindset?

c What advice would you give our readers?

d How can you develop a growth mindset?

3 **Read the interview again and circle the correct answers.**

1 Even if you have a fixed mindset, you …
  - a never change.
  - b are bad at maths.
  - c can change.
  - d like taking tests.

2 People with a growth mindset …
  - a think they can get better.
  - b are good at everything.
  - c are scared of failing.
  - d don't have to learn new skills.

3 Malcolm …
  - a wanted to learn the piano.
  - b played the piano for several years.
  - c learned to play the guitar easily.
  - d slowly improved his guitar playing.

4 Malcolm encourages readers to …
  - a learn from their mistakes.
  - b wait before trying new things.
  - c ignore their mistakes.
  - d try one thing at a time.

4 **Find words in the interview that mean:**

1 a feeling/opinion (question 1) ________

2 not changing (question 1) ________

3 without purpose (question 2) ________

4 necessary (question 4) ________

5 not a success (question 4) ________

The power of 'not yet'

Imagine you've just failed an important maths test. What do you think?

a I failed this test, but I can pass the next one if I study harder.

b I'm just not good at maths. There's no point trying.

If you chose a, you have a growth mindset. People with a growth mindset are often happier and more successful. But if you chose b, don't worry – you can change. I spoke to psychologist Malcolm Adams to find out how.

1 ☐ A mindset is your attitude to life. Some people have a fixed mindset. These people often avoid trying new things because they're afraid of making mistakes. They refuse to try harder, because they don't believe they can get better. On the other hand, people with a growth mindset believe they can improve with practice. They're eager to learn new skills and they're not afraid to fail sometimes. They often do well in life.

2 ☐ Let me tell you a story to explain this. When I was a kid my parents made me learn the piano. I didn't like the piano and it was really difficult. I remember feeling annoyed with myself whenever I made a mistake. After about a year, I stopped trying. I thought, 'This is pointless. I don't have any musical talent.'

3 ☐ Exactly. But later, at university, a friend said to me, 'If you want to be good at something, you have to believe you can do it.' So I thought, 'OK, let's try again.' I decided to learn the guitar, which I'd always adored. This time I told myself, 'You can do it!' I practised loads. It was hard, but little by little I got better. I'll never forget playing for my friends for the first time. I was thrilled! My mindset had completely changed.

4 ☐ Firstly, believe in yourself. Being positive is essential. Secondly, don't worry about making mistakes. A mistake isn't failure – it's an opportunity to learn. Finally, don't forget to use the power of 'not yet'. Never say, 'I can't do this.' Always remember to tell yourself, 'I can – just not yet.'

Voice it!

5 **Discuss the questions.**

1 Do you like to try new things? Why / Why not?

2 Where do you think you are on the scale for the activities in the box? Why? How can you change?

> doing art   doing sports
> playing music and singing   speaking English

1 ↑ fixed mindset
2
3 a mixture of both
4
5 ↓ growth mindset

Finished? p124 Ex 1

LANGUAGE IN ACTION
Gerunds and infinitives

Watch video 7.2
Why does Claire inspire him?
What did he try last summer?

Gerunds		Infinitives (with *to*)	
As the subject of the sentence	[1]Being positive is essential.	To explain purpose	[2]I spoke to Malcolm Adams to find out how.
After prepositions	[3]They're afraid of making mistakes.	After adjectives	[4]They're eager to learn new skills.
After certain verbs (*avoid*, *enjoy*, *finish*, *miss*, etc.)	[5]These people often avoid trying new things.	After certain verbs (*hope*, *refuse*, *would like*, etc.)	[6]They refuse to try harder.

1 **Underline the gerunds and infinitives (with *to*) in the examples in the table above.**

Get it right!

Some verbs, including *like*, *love* and *start*, can take the gerund or infinitive with no change in meaning.

*He **loves going/to go** for walks.*

2 **Complete the text with the gerund or infinitive form of the verbs in the box.**

develop feel help (x2) increase ~~know~~ make say

THINK POSITIVE

You'll be glad [1] *to know* there are steps you can take [2] ________ a positive mindset. Psychologists suggest [3] ________ a list of activities that make you feel good, and then doing one every day [4] ________ your positivity. [5] ________ others when they have a problem also makes us feel happier. Of course, it's important [6] ________ thank you to people for [7] ________ you. Try it! Everyone wants [8] ________ more satisfied in life.

You can use the gerund or infinitive after *remember*, *forget* and *stop*, but this changes the meaning.

Gerunds	Infinitives (with *to*)
I **remember feeling** annoyed. *(= I have a memory of …)*	Always **remember to tell** yourself … *(= don't forget)*
I'll never **forget playing** for my friends for the first time. *(= I won't forget that memory)*	Don't **forget to use** the power of 'not yet'. *(= don't forget to do this in the future)*
I **stopped trying**. *(= I didn't do this anymore)*	I **stopped to rest** for a few minutes. *(= I stopped what I was doing for a while)*

3 **Complete the questions with the gerund or infinitive form of the verbs in brackets.**

1 Do you remember *meeting* (meet) your best friend?
2 When you're studying, how often do you stop ________ (take) a break?
3 What would happen if you forgot ________ (set) your alarm the night before an exam?
4 Would it be harder to stop ________ (use) your phone?
5 What things do you have to remember ________ (do) this weekend?
6 Think of two people you'll never forget ________ (meet) on your first day at school. Who are they?

Use it!

4 **Ask and answer the questions in Exercise 3.**

Finished? p124 Ex 2

VOCABULARY AND LISTENING

Expressions with *heart* and *mind*

7.04 **1 Match the phrases in bold in the thought bubbles with definitions a–j. Listen, check and repeat.**

I have to [1]**learn by heart** so many facts for that exam but I don't have time!

What am I going to study at university? I have to [2]**make my mind up** soon.

I'm [3]**in two minds** about the party. I don't know many people there. Shall I go or just stay home?

[4]**I've got something on my mind** about school. Who should I talk to?

I want to become an actor, but what will Dad say? It'll [5]**break his heart** if I don't study science.

Education is a subject that's [6]**close to my heart**, but I don't know if I'd be a good teacher or not!

I need to choose my degree carefully. I can't [7]**change my mind** later.

I know if I [8]**put my heart into** this project, I'll do well, but I'm so tired!

It's just [9]**crossed my mind** that Dan might be at the party.

I must [10]**bear in mind** we can't use a pencil in the exam. I don't want to fail for something silly like that!

a consider something important 10
b make an effort to do something ☐
c think of something ☐
d make a decision ☐
e memorise ☐
f change a decision ☐
g unable to decide between two options ☐
h be worried about something ☐
i make someone really sad ☐
j be important to someone ☐

LEARN TO LEARN

Gapped flashcards

Flashcards can help you learn expressions.

2 Make flashcards for some of the expressions in Exercise 1, leaving a gap for *heart* or *mind*(*s*). Write the missing word on the back. Then test your partner.

be in two ______ | minds

Use it!

3 Choose six phrases in Exercise 1 and make sentences with the ideas in the box.

clothes | friends and family | going out

When I go out in the evening, I have to bear in mind what time my parents want me to come home.

A conversation

4 Which of these things do you think can reduce exam stress?

1 studying late at night
2 studying with friends
3 drinking energy drinks
4 doing exercise
5 testing yourself
6 eating apples
7 making lists

7.05 **5 Listen to the conversation. Circle the things in Exercise 4 that the counsellor recommends.**

7.05 **6 Listen again and discuss the questions.**

1 Why is Gavin so stressed?
He's worried he's going to fail his exams.
2 Why does the counsellor suggest making a list?
3 Why does the counsellor recommend eating apples and nuts?
4 Why doesn't Gavin want to go to bed early?
5 Why is it important for Gavin to do well in every subject?
6 What is Gavin going to ask his sister tonight?
7 What was Gavin in two minds about earlier?

7 Do you think the counsellor's suggestions are useful?

LANGUAGE IN ACTION
Subject and object questions

Watch video 7.3
What's good about keeping a journal? Who helped her today?

Subject questions	
Who helps you?	My sister (helps me).
[1]________ makes you think that?	Everything (makes me think that)!
Object questions	
Who do you want to teach?	(I want to teach) primary school kids.
[2]________ she study?	(She studied) physics.

1 Complete the examples in the table above.

2 Circle the correct words to complete the rules.

1. The words in red are *subjects / objects.* The ones in green are *subjects / objects*.
2. *Subject / Object* questions always use a form of *do*.

3 Complete the present simple questions with subject or object question forms.

1. What do you do (do/you) at the weekend?
2. Who ________ (teach) you maths?
3. Who ________ (send) you the most messages every day?
4. Which subjects ________ (put/you) your heart into?
5. Who ________ (help) you with your homework?
6. What ________ (happen) if you don't sleep enough?

4 Complete the past simple questions with subject or object question forms.

1. Who taught (teach) you English last year?
2. What ________ (eat / you) for breakfast?
3. Who ________ (give) you presents for your birthday?
4. What presents ________ (give / they) you?
5. Which TV shows ________ (watch / you) yesterday?
6. Which country ________ (win) the last football World Cup?

5 Ask and answer the questions in Exercises 2 and 3.

6 Complete the dialogue with the correct subject or object question form. Listen and check. 7.06

OLAF What's that?
ROSA It's a stress ball.
OLAF What [1]does it do (do/it)?
ROSA It helps you relax. Look, you squeeze it like this. It was a birthday present.
OLAF Wow, that feels great! Who [2]________ (give) it to you?
ROSA My sister. She knows I get stressed out a lot so she thought it might help.
OLAF I want one.
ROSA You don't need one! You never get stressed.
OLAF That's not true. Who [3]________ (tell) you that? I get stressed before exams.
ROSA Well, you could borrow this one if you like.
OLAF No, I'd prefer my own, thanks. Where [4]________ (get/ your sister) it?
ROSA Online, I think.
OLAF What site [5]________ (use/she)? Do you know?
ROSA I'll ask her, but I'm sure you can get them in lots of places. They've been around for years.
OLAF Really? Who [6]________ (invent) them?
ROSA No idea. Let's look it up!

Use it!

7 Ask and answer the questions.

1. Who did you call/visit/help yesterday?
2. Who called/visited/helped you yesterday?

Pronunciation p142

Finished? p124 Ex 3

SPEAKING

Expressing sympathy and concern

1 What problems do brothers and sisters usually have?

7.10 **2 Listen to the conversation. What is Jerry's problem?**

PAULA Hey, Jerry. What's [1] the matter ? You look really down.
JERRY I am. It's my brother. He's refusing to talk to me.
PAULA Really? That's not [2] ________ . Why?
JERRY His tablet has stopped working. He thinks I took it without asking and broke it, but I didn't, I swear. Now when I try to talk to him he just walks away.
PAULA That's a little harsh, isn't it?
JERRY The thing is, he ought to know I wouldn't take his stuff without permission. I feel really hurt.
PAULA I [3] ________ . It's horrible when someone doesn't believe you. But bear in mind he's doing his final exams at the moment. He's probably really stressed out about everything.
JERRY I guess you're right, but I hope he calms down soon.
PAULA Is there [4] ________ ? I have an old tablet I could lend him.
JERRY That's kind of you, but you don't need to do that.
PAULA Don't mention it, but let me know if you change your mind. It'll [5] ________ .

7.10 **3 Complete the conversation with the phrases from the *Useful language* box. Listen and check.**

Useful language

I can imagine.	That's not very nice.
Is there anything I can do to help?	What's the matter?
It'll all be OK, you'll see.	

4 Replace the phrases in bold with the *Everyday English* phrases in the box.

1 Do I need help? No, **that's a nice thing to offer**, but I'm fine. ________
2 **I'm absolutely certain** my keys are here. I had them a few minutes ago. ________
3 Your teacher told you off for being two minutes late? That's **not fair**. ________
4 Of course you're **totally nervous and worried**. It's your final exams! ________
5 A Thanks for letting me use your desk.
B **No problem at all**. ________

Watch video 7.4
Everyday English

a little harsh — Don't mention it. — I swear — stressed out — That's kind of you …

PLAN

5 Make notes about one of the problems you thought of in Exercise 1.

____
____
____

SPEAK

6 Practise talking about the problem with your partner. Remember to use gerunds or infinitives, vocabulary from this unit and phrases from the *Useful language* and *Everyday English* boxes

CHECK

7 Work with another pair. Listen to their conversation and complete the notes.

What problem did they talk about? ________
____

How sympathetic did the conversation sound?
____

WRITING
An email reply

1 **Look at the photo of a teenager and her mum. What do you think is the problem?**

2 **Read the email to a teenage magazine and the reply. Who is asking for advice? Who is giving it?**

Dear Abby,
I want to follow my daughter on social media because I'm worried about who she might become friends with, but she says I can't because it would be 'totally embarrassing' if I posted on her wall. I feel hurt by her reaction. You're a teenager – how can I change her mind?
Many thanks,
Janelle

Dear Janelle,
I'm glad you wrote. Firstly, this is a common problem, so don't feel down. However, your daughter's reaction isn't unusual. It doesn't mean she doesn't love you, but she needs space.
I would recommend telling her why you are worried. It would definitely help to talk. Why don't you suggest following, her but promise not to post on her wall? If she isn't happy with that, it might be better not to follow her at all. Whatever you do, don't get annoyed with her and don't forget to tell her that you trust her.
Good luck, and let me know how it goes.
Abby

3 **How useful is Abby's advice?**

4 **Look at the *Useful language* box. Find and underline the phrases in Abby's email.**

5 **Complete the mini-dialogues with the phrases from the *Useful language* box.**

1 A So the party starts at seven, does it?
B Yes, but ________________, don't tell Pablo. It's a surprise.

2 A My best friend is stressed about her exams.
B ________________ joining a study group?

3 A Joe has to take his medicine.
B Yes, but ________________ not to wake him. He needs to rest as well.

4 A What's a good way to get fit and have fun?
B ________________ joining a football team.

5 A Felix isn't talking to me.
B Well, ________________ say sorry.

Useful language

It might be better (not) to …
It would definitely help to …
I would recommend … (+ *-ing*)
Whatever you do, don't …
Why don't you suggest … (+ *-ing*)?

Write an email reply to a worried parent.

PLAN

6 **Imagine you are Abby. Choose one of the problems below to reply to. Think of three pieces of advice that they should or shouldn't do.**

My son never does his homework on time. His teachers are angry and I don't know what to do.

My daughter refuses to help with the housework. She says she's too busy studying.

WRITE

7 **Write your email reply. Remember to include the plan in Exercise 6, language from this unit and phrases from the *Useful language* box.**

CHECK

8 **Do you …**

- say what the person should do?
- say what the person should not do?
- think the advice is useful?

Finished? p124 Ex 4

AROUND THE WORLD

READING

A report about schools in Denmark

Globetrotters

Watch video 7.5
Happiness around the world

- What different things can make us happy?
- Are Costa Rica and Norway considered happy countries? Why?
- What do Ecuador and Bhutan have in common?

1 **What do you think is most important in making a school a happy place? Why?**

a lots of events
b a nice building
c student clubs and sports teams
d technology in the classroom

7.11 2 **Read the report and put the paragraph titles in the correct place 1–5. Listen and check your answers.**

a Enjoying *hygge* is for everyone
b Conclusion
c Introduction
d Understanding other people
e Learning with others builds a better society

The happiest children in the world: a report

1 ☐

We have written this report to describe some of the reasons why Danish children are the happiest in the world. It is part of our school project 'Happier students, happier societies'.

2 ☐

One of the most important reasons Danish children are so happy is that they are taught empathy from a very young age. Empathy is the ability to imagine what it must be like to be another person. At preschool, Danish children learn to do this by studying facial expressions. They are shown pictures of the faces of other children showing anger, fear, sadness, etc. The preschool children say what they think the children in the pictures are feeling, and try to imagine being them. Schoolchildren never stop learning about empathy. Even 15- and 16-year-olds continue to have one hour a week of empathy as a compulsory subject.

3 ☐

Danish teenagers also have 'Class time'. This is a special time when students come together to talk about any individual or group problems they are having. This could be a personal issue between two students, or even something unrelated to school. During this time, everyone bears in mind the feelings of others and avoids criticising anyone. The group tries to find a solution together. They do this in a peaceful environment, with everyone glad to take part. 'Class time' is connected to *hygge*, a Danish word that is tricky to translate into English but which means relaxed and cosy.

4 ☐

In Danish schools students with different strengths and weaknesses study together in mixed groups. This helps to develop their empathy by showing them that everyone has strong points, talents and positive qualities. One student might find English difficult, for example, but be good at maths. Another might find English easy but find it difficult to understand maths. In a Danish school, these two students would help each other during lessons, and often between lessons as well. The system develops teamwork, respect and collaboration. These are essential qualities for a successful, happy life both at school and in the adult world.

5 ☐

In summary, the main reason that Danish children are so happy is very simple: they develop empathy, and empathy increases happiness by making everyone feel included and understood. They do this in a number of different but connected ways: learning to read the feelings of others, discussing problems together, and working in mixed groups. We believe that introducing any one of these methods into our own school would be straightforward and would improve our school life a great deal. Imagine what we could achieve if we tried all three!

3 **Read the report again and circle the correct answers.**

1 This report was written by …
 a teachers.
 b students.

2 Preschool Danish children look at pictures of …
 a their classmates.
 b children they don't know.

3 Danish teenagers …
 a can study empathy if they want to.
 b have to study empathy.

4 In 'Class time' students talk about …
 a all kinds of problems.
 b their individual problems.

5 In Danish schools, students with different abilities …
 a help each other in class.
 b help each other in and out of class.

6 To improve their own school, the writers suggest …
 a trying all the ideas in the report.
 b trying only one of the ideas.

LEARN TO LEARN

Synonyms and antonyms

Learning words with similar or opposite meanings can help you to increase your vocabulary quickly.

4 **Complete the table with words from the report.**

	Word(s) with a similar meaning	Word with the opposite meaning
joy	happiness	1 sadness
2	obligatory	optional
3	single	4
related	5	6
difficult	7	easy
8	strong points	weaknesses
important	9	unimportant
simple	10	complicated

Voice it!

5 **Discuss the questions.**

1 Which of the ideas in the report do you think is best for developing empathy? Why?

2 Why is empathy important in life?

Explore it!

Guess the correct answer.

Which of these can make you happier?

a smelling flowers
b the colour yellow
c being outside

Find another interesting fact about happiness. Write a question for your partner to answer.

OWN IT! The Culture Project Teacher's Resource Bank

7 REVIEW

VOCABULARY

1 Circle the correct words.

Hi Lee,

How's it going? I've been in Turkey for a month. I'm [1]*glad / hopeful* I came to a town and not a city. It's more [2]*peaceful / grateful*. I've been practising Turkish a lot – you know me, I'm [3]*eager / insecure* to learn! I felt [4]*satisfied / ridiculous* at first, but I'm improving. I'm [5]*thrilled / annoyed* when people understand me, although sometimes people are [6]*hurt / amused* by my mistakes. Mehmet has introduced me to lots of people. I'm really [7]*grateful / down* to him.

Anyway, how are you? Write soon!

James

2 Complete the sentences with an expression with *heart* or *mind*.

1. I'm ______________ about the party. Should I go or not?
2. Waiter! I've ______________ . I'll have pizza, not pasta.
3. My sister's great at ______________ all sorts of facts and dates ______________ .
4. Pollution is an issue that's really ______________ . That's why I don't drive.
5. It takes me ages ______________ what to wear in the morning. I'd prefer a school uniform!
6. Can I talk to you? I've got ______________ . It's about my best friend.

LANGUAGE IN ACTION

3 Complete the sentences with the gerund or infinitive with *to* form of the verbs in brackets.

1. I'm not shy about ________ (give) presentations.
2. I was so glad ________ (see) my cousin at the party.
3. I remember ________ (feel) really insecure on my first day at school.
4. My baby brother is always amused at something. He never stops ________ (laugh).
5. ________ (keep) notes of new vocabulary is really important when you study.

4 Complete the dialogue with the correct subject and object questions.

EMMA Happy birthday!
YUSUF Thanks, guys! This is amazing. Who [1]__________ (cook) the cake?
TIM Emma did.
YUSUF It's delicious. What [2]__________ (put/you) in it, Emma?
EMMA Sorry – that's a secret! Anyway, what [3]__________ (think) of your birthday playlist?
YUSUF I love it. Who [4]__________ (make) it?
TIM Emma put it together.
YUSUF Who [5]__________ (choose) the song that's playing now? It's one of my favourites.
TIM That was me!
EMMA So tell us – what presents [6]__________ (get/you)?
YUSUF Some clothes and this fidget spinner.
TIM Who [7]__________ (give) you that?
YUSUF My cousin. He knows I collect them.
TIM What [8]__________ (want/you) to drink? Some juice, some cola? We've got everything.

Self-assessment

I can use adjectives to talk about feelings.

I can use expressions with *heart* and *mind*.

I can use gerunds and infinitives.

I can use subject and object questions.

LEARN TO ... GIVE YOUR PARTNER USEFUL FEEDBACK

You can help your partner to improve their speaking by giving useful feedback. When you work together, they can help you improve too.

1 **Match 1–5 with a–e to complete advice about giving feedback.**

Giving your partner feedback can help them speak, but there are some important things to bear in mind.

1 Being positive is important, so always tell your partner ______
2 You don't want your partner to feel hurt, so ______
3 Remember to focus on their English and avoid ______
4 Feedback should be useful, so don't forget ______
5 Be honest. Don't say something is ______

a talking about personal things.
b to give ideas for how your partner can improve.
c talk about anything negative in a friendly way.
d better or worse than it really is.
e what you liked and what they did well.

2 **Look at the feedback that seven students have given Lars. Do they follow the advice in Exercise 1? Why? / Why not?**

1 *You didn't speak very clearly. You sounded like a robot!*

2 *I'm glad you used lots of the new vocabulary. That was nice!*

3 *You've got a gorgeous voice!*

4 *You repeated some words a lot. I would recommend using synonyms next time.*

5 *You made some grammar mistakes, but maybe because you were nervous.*

6 *That was absolutely the most dreadful presentation in history!*

7 *I think you'll sound more natural next time if you don't learn everything by heart.*

3 **Prepare a talk about a topic in the box.**

a happy memory
growth mindset
how to deal with exam stress
how to stay happy

OWN IT!

4 **Take turns to give your talks. While your partner is speaking, think about these things.**

- What do you like about their talk?
- What language do they use well?
- How can they improve next time?

5 **Give your partner useful feedback using the advice in Exercise 1. Is your partner's feedback on your own talk useful? How?**

8 ADVERTISING

LEARNING OUTCOMES

I can …

- understand texts about online advertising and social media influencers
- recommend an online tool
- write an online product review
- understand how to use defining and non-defining relative clauses, and indefinite, reflexive and reciprocal pronouns
- talk about advertising and use Internet verbs
- understand word building (nouns and verbs) and how to answer open-ended questions
- create an advert storyboard.

Start it!

1 Look at the photo. Is there a place where you live where you can see lots of adverts like this?
2 Before you watch, think of all the different places where you can see adverts.
3 What are the four important aspects of advertising? Watch and check.
4 What's your favourite advert? Why?

Watch video 8.1

p97

Language in action 8.2

p99

Language in action 8.3

p100

Everyday English 8.4

VOCABULARY
Advertising

8.01 **1 Read the story of an advert and put pictures A–F in the correct order. Listen and repeat the words in bold.**

1 ___ 2 ___ 3 ___
4 ___ 5 ___ 6 ___

8.02 **2 Circle the correct words. Listen and check.**

1 I love watching funny *marketing companies* / *adverts* online or on TV.
2 My dad always buys the same *brand* / *product* of toothpaste.
3 Sometimes it's not easy for *sellers* / *buyers* to decide which product they want.
4 I always look at *ad blockers* / *reviews* before I buy something new.
5 That advert *advertised* / *influenced* my decision to buy a new tablet.
6 At school we have to draw a simple design for a *logo* / *slogan* competition.

LEARN TO LEARN
Wordbuilding: nouns and verbs

When you learn a noun, check the verb form and record them in a table.

3 Complete the table.

Noun	Verb
advert	[1] advertise
product	[2]
[3]	buy
review	[4]
[5]	block (an ad)
[6]	market
influencer	[7]
seller	[8]

4 Close your books. One person says a noun from the table and the other says the matching verb.

ADVERTISING A PRODUCT

First, a company makes something to sell. This is the **product**. Then, they create a **brand** to represent the product – this is a name and design that creates a product's identity. It is usually represented by a symbol or **logo**. There is often a **slogan** (a short phrase that is easy to remember) linked to a brand.

Next an **advert** is made to **advertise** the product. This could be a poster in the street or a short film on the television or online that shows what the product is like. It is made by a **marketing company** to encourage or **influence** people to buy the product.

When the product goes on sale the customer or **buyer** buys the product from a **seller**. Buyers sometimes write their opinions about the product in an online **review**. People who don't want to see online adverts use an **ad blocker**, a computer programme that stops adverts appearing on the screen.

Use it!

5 Read the questions and make notes.

1 Do you think ad blockers are a good idea? Why?
2 Do online reviews influence people to buy a product?
3 Which brand slogans or logos can you remember?

6 Ask and answer the questions in Exercise 5.

Explore it!

Guess the correct answer.

When you see a glass of milk in an advert, it probably isn't milk. What is it?

a paint b glue c yoghurt

Find out some tricks that are used in adverts to make products look good. Write a question for your partner to answer.

READING

A report

8.03 **1 What can you see in the photos? What do you think people do with the videos? Read the report and check your ideas.**

2 Read the report again. What do the numbers refer to?

1 31% ________________
2 74% ________________
3 +600 million ________________

3 Which type of advertising do the sentences refer to: *I* (influencer, *UGC* (user-generated content) or *N* (native)?

1 Customers can win prizes. ___
2 Customers share photos of themselves. ___
3 It doesn't look like advertising. ___
4 People buy the products to copy someone else. ___
5 Products are promoted by famous people. ___
6 There is a word that tells you it's an advert. ___

4 Find words in the report that mean:

1 people who follow someone online (I) ________
2 a planned series of activities to advertise a product (UGC) ________
3 something that has your name on (UGC) ________
4 to stop (N) ________
5 paid advertising (N) ________

Voice it!

5 Discuss the questions.

1 Do you have a favourite social media influencer or vlogger?
2 Where have you seen native ads on social media?

Online advertising

Social media influencers

One of the most successful types of advertising on social media is influencer advertising. Brands choose social media stars who have thousands of followers on their blog, YouTube channel or Instagram to advertise their products. The stars talk positively about the products in a natural, personal way, which is different to the slogans in traditional adverts. They might talk about a beauty product, play a song, or wear certain clothes in their videos, photos or blogs. Many fans, who want to copy their favourite social media stars, go and buy the same products when they see them.

What influences us to buy a product?
Shop websites – 56%, Brand websites – 34%, Blogs – 31%

User-generated content

Another technique used is user-generated content, or UGC. You may know a soft drinks company whose advertising campaign put everyday names on their drinks bottles. Buyers took photos of themselves with their personalised bottle and shared them on social media. With UGC the buyer becomes the person who advertises the brand so, for example, they upload photos of themselves wearing clothes with the brand logo. Sometimes companies have competitions where you can win a prize for the best photo, and of course, it's free advertising for the brand.

Who gives you the best product information?
(Traditional media) TV – 34%, radio – 37%, newspapers – 44%,
(UGC) social networking – 50%, reviews – 68%, conversations with friends – 74%

Native advertising

Have you ever used an ad blocker so you don't see so many adverts online? Ad blockers block some adverts, but not native advertising. It's a type of advertising that you can't see because it looks exactly the same as a social platform or website. For example, on Facebook a native ad looks like a normal post with like, share and comment buttons, or it could be a photo or video on Instagram. However, if you look closely, you will see the words 'sponsored' or 'paid post' next to it. The good thing about native advertising is that users don't feel like their favourite social media channels are full of adverts, but some people don't like the idea of hidden adverts.

Fact: +600M people use ad blockers

Pronunciation p142

Finished? p125 Ex 1

LANGUAGE IN ACTION

Defining and non-defining relative clauses

Watch video 8.2
What is he giving advice about?
What should you do with your phone?

Defining relative clauses
With UGC the buyer becomes the person [1]________ / **that** advertises the brand.
It's a type of advertising **which** / [2]________ you can't see.
Sometimes companies have competitions [3]________ you can win a prize for the best photo.
Many fans buy the same products [4]________ they see them.
You may know a soft drinks company [5]________ advertising campaign put everyday names on their drinks bottles.
Non-defining relative clauses
The stars talk positively about the products in a natural, personal way, [6]________ is different to the slogans in traditional adverts.
Many fans, [7]________ want to copy their favourite social media stars, go and buy the same products when they see them.

1 Complete the examples in the table above. Use the report on page 96 to help you.

2 Circle the correct relative pronouns.

1. The online advertising *who* / *which* most teens prefer is made by social media influencers.
2. Influencers *that* / *whose* channels have the most followers advertise lots of products.
3. Some influencers *who* / *where* advertise products are paid lots of money.
4. Many teens ignore adverts *which* / *when* they see them on social networking sites.
5. Marketing companies look for sites online *which* / *where* they can advertise products.

Use it!

3 Complete the sentences with the relative pronouns in the box and your own ideas.

when	which	whose

1. A time ________ I feel happy is ____________________.
2. Someone ________ videos I have watched is ____________________.
3. The apps ________ I use most are ____________________.

4 Join the two sentences with a relative pronoun.

1. Jo has got her own vlog. Jo is older than me. (who)
   Jo, who's older than me, has got her own vlog.
2. We're going on holiday to the beach. Katia's family have got a house at the beach. (where)
   ____
3. My phone takes excellent photos. My phone is really old. (which)
   ____

Use it!

5 Think of six quiz questions about facts you have read in this book. Use a relative clause.

What was the name of the person who … ?

6 Ask and answer your questions.

Finished? p125 Ex 2

VOCABULARY AND LISTENING

Internet verbs

8.06 **1 Match words 1–10 with definitions a–j. Listen and repeat the words in bold.**

- I [1]**subscribe to** a YouTube channel about parkour. They [2]**post** some awesome videos on it.
- If your Internet doesn't work, [3]**switch** it **off** and then [4]**switch** it **on** again.
- My sister didn't [5]**build up** many followers on Twitter so she [6]**shut down** her account.
- You should [7]**follow** Zoella. She [8]**vlog**s about loads of interesting things and I love her recipes.
- If people [9]**comment on** the post and it isn't very nice, we [10]**delete** it.

a choose to see the things someone uploads on social media 7
b close or stop something ☐
c increase the number of something ☐
d make and share videos online ☐
e put a message or image on social media ☐
f remove something ☐
g start something working ☐
h stop something working ☐
i write your opinion online ☐
j agree to regularly receive an online service or information about it ☐

Use it!

2 Ask and answer questions. Find three things you have in common.

commented on something	deleted something
followed someone	posted something
subscribed to a channel	vlogged about something

Have you ever followed someone on social media?

Yes, of course!

Who do you follow?

I follow all my friends and some celebrities online.

An interview

8.07 **3 Jerome is an influencer. Put the events in the order you think he did them. Listen to the interview and check your answers.**

a He tried out and reviewed products. ☐
b He commented on other posts. ☐
c He got 10,000 followers. ☐
d He posted videos every day. ☐
e He set up his own YouTube channel. ☐

LEARN TO LEARN

Open-ended questions

Read open-ended questions before you listen and think of possible answers. As you listen, make notes of important words, (names, numbers, etc.).

4 Discuss the questions in Exercise 5. Think of possible answers for each question.

Jerome wanted to talk about a hobby, teach people about something or show people how to make something.

8.07 **5 Listen again and answer the questions.**

1 Why did Jerome start a YouTube channel?
Because he wanted to talk about gaming.
2 Why did he delete his videos at first?
______
3 What did his followers like about his vlogs?
______
4 Why did he nearly shut down his account?
______
5 How did he solve the problem?
______
6 When did companies send him new games?
______
7 What advice does he give?
______

6 Would you like to be an influencer? Why? / Why not?

LANGUAGE IN ACTION

Indefinite, reflexive and reciprocal pronouns

Indefinite pronouns
Give your followers **something** new. **No one** is interested in your selfies. Have you got any advice for **anyone**? There weren't any comments from [1] ________ . I think that's why **everyone** likes it so much.
Reflexive pronouns
I tried the game out **myself**. People are interested in [2] ________ .
Reciprocal pronouns
Some followers started arguing with **each other** / **one another**.

Get it right!

*They looked at **themselves** in the mirror.*
(Each person looked at himself/herself.)
*They looked at **each other**.*
(They looked at the different people in the group.)

1 Complete the examples in the table above.

2 Circle the correct indefinite pronouns.

1 Has *anybody* / *nobody* seen this funny video?
2 I've looked *everywhere* / *somewhere* for my mobile, but I can't find it *anywhere* / *somewhere*.
3 *Anyone* / *No one* commented on *anything* / *everything* she said.
4 We're going *everywhere* / *somewhere* in the centre of town for *everything* / *something* to eat.
5 Are you doing *anything* / *everything* special for your birthday?

3 Complete the sentences with reflexive pronouns.

1 She taught ________ how to set up a website.
2 We really enjoyed ________ at the party.
3 He's selfish. He only thinks about ________ .
4 I love taking selfies of ________ .

Watch video 8.3
How many followers do micro-influencers have? Why are they better than celebrity influencers?

4 Match 1–4 with a–d. Then make sentences with *each other* / *one another*.

1 My brother lives in the USA so we talk to
2 We talk a lot. We're always sending
3 We haven't seen
4 They don't understand

a and argue all the time.
b for ages.
c messages.
d with a webcam.

1 My brother lives in the USA so we talk to each other / one another with a webcam.
2 ________________
3 ________________
4 ________________

5 8.08 Circle the correct words to complete the text. Listen and check.

Ads are [1] *everywhere* / *anywhere*, but have you ever asked [2] *ourself* / *yourself* how advertising works? Marketing companies use techniques to make us buy things we don't even want. [3] *Everything* / *Nothing* is more effective than making us think that we are missing out on [4] *something* / *anything* that [5] *everyone* / *no one* else has and that we will be happier if we buy [6] *ourselves* / *themselves* something new. They also make us compare [7] *myself* / *ourselves* to others. For example, in a typical shampoo ad, two women look at [8] *themselves* / *each other*. One of them asks herself, 'Why is her hair so beautiful?' When they talk to [9] *one another* / *themselves* she discovers the secret: The incredible shampoo!

Use it!

6 Complete the sentences so they are true for you.

1 I have taught myself to ________________ .
2 I never go anywhere without ________________ .

Finished? p125 Ex 3

SPEAKING

Recommending an online tool

8.09 **1 Listen to the conversation. What problem does Niall have? What does Ginny recommend?**

8.09 **2 Complete the conversation with the phrases from the *Useful language* box. Listen and check.**

GINNY What's up, Niall?
NIALL I've got to make a video for my technology project to advertise something and I don't have a clue what to do. [1] I don't know where to start ! Can you think of anything?
GINNY [2] ______________ use a video creation tool. [3] ______________ to make videos. I've used some great ones. There are loads of options online.
NIALL That sounds like a plan. What do I need to know?
GINNY Well, a video creation tool [4] ______________ because it would provide you with a ready-made template.
NIALL [5] ______________ ?
GINNY Yeah, you can teach yourself to do it, no problem.
NIALL Excellent! So I add my own text and images, do I?
GINNY Well, you need to write your own text, but most video creation tools have a ready-made image bank, which is handy.
NIALL Great, I can use their images.
GINNY Yep and you can add music and a voiceover. [6] ______________ !
NIALL Sounds like a no-brainer. I'll check out the options online. Thanks, Ginny!

Useful language

I can't recommend it/them enough!
I don't know where to start!
Is it easy to use?
It's the best thing …
(It) would be ideal …
You really ought to …

3 Match the *Everyday English* phrases with the meanings 1–4. How do you say these phrases in your language?

1 useful ______________
2 I have no idea. ______________
3 What's the matter? / How are you? ______________
4 obviously the right choice ______________

Watch video 8.4
Everyday English

handy I don't have a clue. no-brainer What's up?

PLAN

4 Make notes about an online tool you want to recommend. Use the ideas below or your own ideas.

an app a comic maker a music video creator a presentation tool

____
____
____

SPEAK

5 Practise recommending the tool to your partner. Remember to use language from this unit and phrases from the *Useful language* and *Everyday English* boxes.

CHECK

6 Work with another pair. Listen to their conversation and complete the notes.

What tool did they talk about? ______________
____

Did they give a good recommendation? ______________
____

HOME | STORIES | PHOTOS

Star rating ★★★★★

1 [ ] ***Sounds Around*** is a great new product. If you're looking for a wireless speaker with a cool design, which is compact in size but big in sound quality, this is for you.

2 [ ] ***Sounds Around*** is designed to be used outside. You can take it everywhere, to the beach, camping or to a pool party. It has all the features you need, it looks great and is extremely tough. One of its best features is that it's waterproof. It also allows you to connect two devices at the same time, so you can choose to play music from either of them. The charging cable is included, but the one thing that's missing is a microphone, so you can't record yourself. However, the battery lasts for 10 hours, which is more than other wireless speakers offered by other brands.

3 [ ] ***Sounds Around*** offers the buyer an excellent range of features at an amazing price. In my opinion it's one of the best low-cost speakers. I can't recommend it enough!

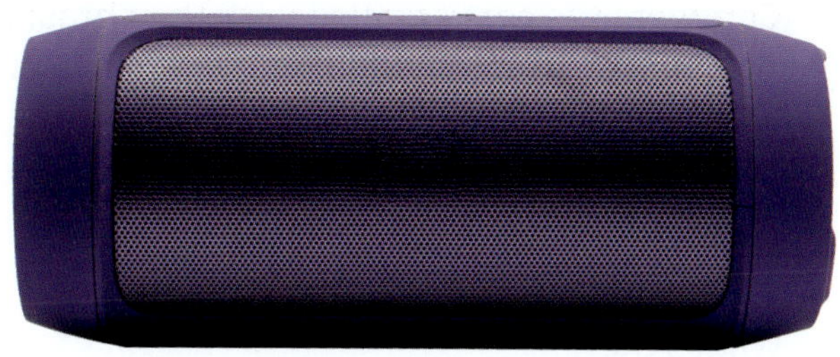

WRITING

An online product review

1 Look at the picture. Which of the features in the box do you think the speaker has? Read the review and check.

compact size   good price   good sound   lightweight   long-lasting battery   microphone   waterproof   wireless

2 Read the review again. Match titles a–c with paragraphs 1–3.

a Opinion
b Short description of the product
c Design and specific features

3 Discuss the questions.

1 Where does the reviewer suggest taking the speaker?
2 What's the advantage of connecting to two devices at the same time?
3 What doesn't the reviewer like about the speaker?
4 Why is the battery better than that of other brands?

4 Read the review again and complete the phrases in the *Useful language* box.

Useful language

1 __________ is included.   It allows you to 2 __________
It is designed to be used 3 __________
One of its best features is 4 __________
The one thing that's missing is 5 __________

Write your own online product review.

PLAN

5 Choose a product to review. Make notes.

short description of the product
design and specific features
your opinion

WRITE

6 Write your product review. Remember to include three paragraphs, language from this unit and phrases from the *Useful language* box.

CHECK

7 Do you …

- give a star rating?
- say what you like and don't like?
- say whether you would buy it?

Finished? p125 Ex 4

THE ART AND DESIGN PROJECT

An advert storyboard

1 **Look at the pictures from an advert. What product does it advertise?**

8.10 **2** **Work in pairs. Look at the pictures and guess the dialogue for each one. Listen and check.**

8.10 **3** **Listen again and complete the table.**

Advert features	Example
1 What's the problem?	*Katia has a backpack that isn't waterproof. When it rains everything gets wet.*
2 What's the solution?	
3 What are the special features of the product?	
4 Who are the characters in the story?	
5 What information does the narrator give?	
6 What's the slogan?	

How to give feedback

4 **Feedback should be positive and useful. Complete the feedback phrases with the words in the box.**

best how idea maybe positive work

The thing I liked [1] ________ was …
Some [2] ________ things were …
I really liked [3] ________ you …
… is a great [4] ________.
[5] ________ you could …
… might [6] ________ too.

A

C

B

D

PLAN

5 Work in groups. Choose a product from the box or your own idea.

sunglasses with headphones personalised trainers a new flavour of soft drink a new perfume

Make a list of its features and the good things about its design. Then create an advert storyboard to advertise the product. Complete the steps below.

- Copy the table in Exercise 3 and complete it with information about your product.
- Write a dialogue and narrator's voiceover.
- Decide how to present the storyboard (act it out, video, poster, slide presentation).
- Work together to prepare your storyboard.
- Practise your presentation.

PRESENT

6 Present your storyboard to your classmates. Remember to use information in Exercises 3 and 5.

CHECK

7 Look at your classmates' storyboard presentations. Give them motivating feedback with the phrases in the *How to* give feedback section. Which advert is your favourite?

8 REVIEW

VOCABULARY

1 Complete the advertising facts with the words in the box.

ad blocker advert advertise brand buyer influence logo marketing company product review seller slogan

Advertising facts

An [1] ______ or ad is a short film, song or picture that tries to make you buy a [2] ______.

When you [3] ______ something you tell people about it to try to sell it.

A [4] ______ is the name you call a product. It is often represented by a symbol or [5] ______.

A [6] ______ buys something from a [7] ______. They sometimes give their opinions about the product in a [8] ______.

When you [9] ______ someone, you change how they think about something.

An [10] ______ is a computer programme that stops adverts appearing on screen.

A [11] ______ is a business that encourages people to buy things.

A [12] ______ is a short phrase used in an advert that is easy to remember.

2 Circle the correct words.

1 Are you going to *post* / *vlog* those photos online?
2 If you don't like comments, you can *subscribe to* / *delete* them.
3 How many people do you *build up* / *follow* online?
4 We have to *switch off* / *shut down* our phones at school.

LANGUAGE IN ACTION

3 Join the sentences to make one sentence with a defining or non-defining relative clause.

1 Pablo is Eva's cousin. Pablo does voiceovers.
______
2 She lent me a book. It didn't have the last page.
______
3 The film was about Corfu. We went to Corfu on holiday.
______
4 Ali is a friend. His wife is an influencer.
______

4 Complete the comments with the words in the box.

each other everyone everything myself ourselves themselves

1 Sometimes images in ads make me feel bad about ______.
2 When we see an ad, we should tell ______ that it's not the real world.
3 ______ sees adverts, but that doesn't mean they believe ______ they see.
4 Many ads show people enjoying ______.
5 Some online ads encourage users to tell ______ about new products.

Self-assessment

I can use words to talk about advertising.

I can use verbs to talk about the Internet.

I can use defining and non-defining relative clauses.

I can use indefinite, reflexive and reciprocal pronouns.

LEARN TO ... WORK OUT THE MEANING OF NEW WORDS

You can work out the meaning of new words and phrases by using clues from the rest of the text.

1 Read the text quickly, ignoring the words in **bold** if you don't understand them. Do you think space advertising is a good idea?

Space advertising

Imagine this. It's 2030 and you're **gazing** up at the night sky. The stars are **twinkling** and the moon is bright, but these days they're **no longer** alone. They've been joined by lots of huge signs in the **darkness**, like the **billboards** you see at the sides of a road, advertising everything from soft drinks to holidays. This might sound like science fiction, but space adverts will be with us **sooner or later**. In fact, a Russian company is already developing the technology to make it possible, and wants to send up its first ads in the next few years.

They will be created by special **satellites**, like the ones that send and receive TV and internet signals, only smaller. These satellites, **arranged** in groups to make the shapes of words or logos, will **reflect** light from the sun and will be **visible** at night from anywhere on Earth. For companies eager to advertise their products to buyers **around the globe**, this might seem like a dream come true. But ask yourself this: shouldn't we keep somewhere free from advertising? After all, ad blockers won't work in space.

2 Three students are working out the meaning of the words in **bold**. Which ones are they talking about?

1 *OK, it's a noun. They must be a kind of advertising sign, because it says you see them at the sides of a road. What else? Well, I know 'board' from 'whiteboard'...*

____

2 *I think this phrase must be about when the ads will be sent up. I know 'soon' and 'late'. They're both about time and they're opposites ...*

____

3 *It's a verb, something that stars do. I think it's connected to their light, because the sentence also says 'and the moon is bright'.*

____

3 What do you think the words mean?

1 ______________
2 ______________
3 ______________

OWN IT!

4 Choose five of the other words or phrases in **bold**. Answer the questions to try to work out their meaning.

1 What is it? A verb, a noun, an adjective or a phrase?
2 What does the rest of the sentence tell you about it?
3 Do you understand part(s) of the word or phrase?
4 What do you think it means?

5 Check the meanings in a dictionary or with your teacher. Were you correct? Did the questions in Exercise 4 help you?

9 HAVE YOU HEARD THE NEWS?

LEARNING OUTCOMES

I can ...

- understand a newspaper story and a news report
- tell an anecdote
- write a news story
- understand how to use reported statements, commands and questions
- use reporting verbs and adverbs of time and manner
- tell stories to remember new verbs, compare notes to improve listening, learn irregular adjective and noun pairs, and practise summarising.

Start it!

1 Look at the photo. What do you think the children are telling each other?
2 Before you watch, why do people like stories?
3 How have Hollywood films and the Internet changed storytelling? Watch and check.
4 Do you like stories with a moral? Why / Why not?

Watch video 9.1

p109

Language in action 9.2

p111

Language in action 9.3

p112

Everyday English 9.4

p114

Globetrotters 9.5

VOCABULARY
Reporting verbs

1 Read news stories A–D. Which one is most interesting? Why?

9.01 2 Match the words in **bold** in the news stories with definitions (a–l). Listen, check and repeat.

A A woman in Georgia, USA [1]**claimed** that she had thrown away jewellery worth $100,000 into the rubbish. The rubbish collection company agreed to look through nearly ten tonnes of rubbish to try and find a black bag with the jewellery. After three hours, they [2]**announced** that they had found it.

a told people officially 2
b said something was true even if it might not be

B A curator at a university in Australia who [3]**insisted** that he should open an old box in a store room [4]**discovered** that it contained an Egyptian mummy that he believes is 2,500 years old. Experts [5]**have confirmed** that the body is an adult and [6]**suggest** that it might be an important woman from ancient Egyptian society.

c have shown that something is true
d found something, especially for the first time
e said something firmly
f mention an idea for others to consider

C A family [7]**have complained** that their neighbours have stolen their cat. However, the neighbours [8]**deny** that they stole the cat and say that it was homeless and hungry, so they gave it food and a home. The neighbours say that the family [9]**refuses** to believe that the cat prefers to live with them!

g say something is not true
h say you will not do something
i have told someone that something is wrong

D A school in the north of England [10]**has apologised** for leaving a teenage student in London after a school trip to the capital city. The school [11]**admitted** that they made a mistake and [12]**promised** that it will never happen again.

j agreed that something was true
k has said sorry for something someone has done
l told someone you will certainly do something

LEARN TO LEARN
Telling stories to remember new words

Use reporting verbs in stories to remember what they mean.

3 Work in pairs.

Student A: Tell your partner one of the stories in Exercise 1. Use reporting verbs, but change one fact.

Student B: Listen to your partner tell the story. What did they change?

Use it!

4 Read the options. Make notes on your answers.

Think of a time when you … something.

1 admitted to ____________
2 denied ____________
3 promised to do ____________
4 apologised for ____________
5 refused to do ____________

5 Compare your answers. Which situations were the most difficult? Which were the easiest?

Explore it!

Guess the correct answer.

In 2014 a French family found a Caravaggio painting in their house. Experts suggested it could be worth … million.

a €20 b €80 c €120

Find an interesting fact about something famous or valuable. Write a question for your partner to answer.

Pronunciation p142

READING

A newspaper story

9.04 **1 Read the newspaper story. Circle the best title.**

a The twins who have never met.

b The twins who have never spent a day apart.

c International twins!

2 Read the newspaper story again and circle the correct answers.

1 Jonas and Santiago have …
   a nothing in common.
   b the same adoptive parents.
   c lots in common.
   d the same school friends.

2 The orphanage … the boys …
   a said … weren't twins.
   b took … to Spain.
   c gave … a blue sweatshirt.
   d suggested … were twins.

3 The twins see each other …
   a every day.
   b as often as possible.
   c only in the USA.
   d only on social media.

4 The boys were filmed …
   a only in Spain.
   b only in the USA.
   c in Spain and the USA.
   d separately.

3 Find words in the story that mean:

1 exactly the same (paragraph 1) ________

2 a home for children whose parents cannot care for them (paragraph 2) ________

3 taken into a different family and looked after (paragraph 2) ________

4 from the same family (paragraph 3) ________

(1) **Identical twins Jonas and Santiago look similar, sound similar and even love the same things. But they live separate lives in different parts of the world and very nearly didn't discover that each other existed.**

(2) In 2004, Jonas and Santiago were left at an orphanage in Ghana, Africa when they were babies. A few months later both boys were adopted but by different families; Jonas by a couple from New York and Santiago by a Spanish family. Fortunately, both families went to collect their baby son at the adoption agency in Ghana on the same day and both had bought a new blue sweatshirt for him to wear. A woman at the adoption agency suggested that the babies looked extremely similar and when the parents saw the two baby boys together in their blue sweatshirts they agreed that they were exactly the same. The parents then discovered that the boys shared the same birthday, but the orphanage denied that they were twins.

(3) The four adoptive parents couldn't believe that the boys weren't related and insisted that they were going to do a DNA test, which confirmed that the boys were in fact identical twins. The parents promised to keep in touch and said that they would meet as soon as they could, which wasn't easy because Santiago lived in a small village in northern Spain and Jonas on the other side of the world in New York.

(4) However, in 2010 they finally met and although they couldn't speak the same language, there was a deep connection between the brothers.

A twin 'can understand you when most people don't,' Jonas said. 'Like in weird situations when you feel a certain way, most people are like, 'What?' But your twin is like, 'Oh, yeah. Yeah, I get that.' I am like, 'Thank you, someone finally gets me.'

(5) Since then, they have seen each other several times and speak online regularly. In an interview, Jonas explained that he had learned some Spanish phrases, such as how to ask for directions, and that Santiago's English had improved dramatically. In 2012 a Spanish film director offered to make a film to tell the boys' story. He suggested filming the boys together in both Spain and the USA. He told the boys to act naturally while he filmed them, so we get to see the boys playing football in the Spanish countryside and going skateboarding and to the cinema in the USA. Jonas admitted that being in a film was 'a bit strange' but 'really fun', especially with his twin brother by his side.

Voice it!

4 Discuss the questions.

1 What is the most amazing thing about their story?

2 What would be difficult about living in a different country to your twin?

3 What would you ask Jonas or Santiago if you met them?

4 Would you like to be a twin? Why / Why not? (If you are a twin, what do / don't you like about it?)

Finished? p126 Ex 1

LANGUAGE IN ACTION

Reported statements and commands

Watch video 9.2
Why did the visitors to the zoo complain? What did the zoo claim?

Statements
The orphanage **denied** (that) they **were** twins.
The parents **insisted** (that) they [1]________ **going to do** a DNA test.
The parents **said** (that) they [2]________ **meet**.
The parents **promised to keep** in touch.
Jonas **explained** (that) Santiago's English [3]________ **improved** dramatically.
Orders / Commands
He [4]________ the boys **to act** naturally.
He **told** me **not to worry**.

1 Complete the examples in the table above. Use the story on page 108 to help you.

Get it right!

After ***tell***, we use words like *the boys*, *me*, etc. and the *to* infinitive.

*She **told him (not) to go**.*

2 Circle the correct words.

The director has agreed [1]*that he makes* / *to make* another film about twins Jonas and Santiago. He explained that the new film [2]*had been* / *would be* about their lives as teenagers and he told us that the boys [3]*were* / *had been* more independent now and that they [4]*were starting* / *to start* to travel between the USA and Spain without their parents. He said that Jonas [5]*lived* / *had been living* with Santiago in Spain and [6]*to go* / *had been* to school with his brother.

3 Complete the reported statements and commands.

1 'I'll do my homework when the film has finished.'
He explained that he …
would do his homework when the film had finished.

2 'I'm going to play your song.'
He promised me that he ________

3 'I didn't take my dad's tablet!'
She denied that she ________

4 'Don't watch this video!'
He told me ________

5 'We will come and meet you at the park.'
They said that they ________

Reported offers and suggestions
A Spanish film director **offered** [1]________ (make) a film to tell the boys' story.
He **suggested** [2]________ (film) the boys together in both Spain and the USA.

4 Complete the examples in the table above with the correct form of the verbs in brackets. Use the story on page 108 to help you.

Use it!

5 Read the dialogue. Write offers and suggestions in reported speech.

SOFIA	Shall we go to the cinema?
PAULA	OK. Let me see what's on.
SOFIA	What about *Horror Fair*?
PAULA	Sounds good.
SOFIA	Shall we go at six o'clock?
PAULA	Sure. I can buy the tickets online.

Sofia suggested going to the cinema later.

____

____

____

____

6 Tell each other the offers and suggestions that Sofia and Paula made.

Finished? p126 Ex 2

LISTENING AND VOCABULARY

A news report

1 **Look at headlines a–c. What do you think the stories are about?**

a Sock horror in girl's bedroom

b **The bird that came back speaking another language**

c Emergency in the kitchen!

9.05 2 **Listen and put the stories in Exercise 1 in the order you hear them.**

1 ___ 2 ___ 3 ___

LEARN TO LEARN

Collaborative listening

Talking about what you understood with a partner before listening a second time can help you find out what you missed.

3 **Tell your partner what you remember about each story. Do you remember the same information?**

9.05 4 **Listen again and answer the questions. Did talking to your partner in Exercise 3 help you?**

1 Where had the parrot been?

____

2 Why did Darren decide not to keep the parrot after he was found?

____

3 What mistake did the girls make?

____

4 What was the emergency?

____

5 Why did the English family make a phone call?

____

6 Why didn't the specialist touch the 'lizard' immediately?

____

Adverbs of time and manner

5 **Read the blog. Which of the two news stories in the blog do you think was invented?**

If you read my blog **regularly**, you'll know I **occasionally** write about 'unbelievable' news stories, like the one about the parrot that spoke Spanish **fluently**. **Nowadays**, there's so much information on the Internet that it's difficult to know if something is true or not. The other day, I was reading a story about a boy who had invented a robot to do his homework. It said he'd been **secretly** developing the technology in his bedroom, **patiently** trying out different designs. Cool idea, right? But the story got **gradually** more ridiculous. It said that one day the robot had offered to go to school, telling the boy he could stay in bed. **After a while**, I began to think, 'This can't be true.' **Eventually**, I realised it was a joke. It's **surprisingly** easy to believe 'fake news'!

9.06 6 **Match the adverbs in bold in the blog with their definitions. Listen, check and repeat.**

1 little by little *gradually* [M]
2 these days ______ [ ]
3 sometimes but not often ______ [ ]
4 in the end ______ [ ]
5 in an unexpected way ______ [ ]
6 without telling anyone ______ [ ]
7 often ______ [ ]
8 in a patient way ______ [ ]
9 easily and well ______ [ ]
10 after some time ______ [ ]

7 **Are the adverbs in Exercise 6 adverbs of time (*T*) or manner (*M*)?**

Use it!

8 **Think of situations when people do things in these ways. Can your partner guess the verb and adverb?**

gradually: get better, move

regularly: go to bed late, not eat, practise

patiently: listen, sit, wait

secretly: gesture, speak, write

This happens before you play an important football match.

You practise regularly?

Yes!

LANGUAGE IN ACTION
Reported questions

Watch video 9.3
What did the two friends want to see?
How did they get into the radio studio?

Direct questions	Reported questions
***Wh-* questions**	
'What **are** your favourite stories?'	Last week, one of our listeners asked us [1]________ our favourite stories **were**.
'Where **did** you **leave** the other sock?'	Everybody asked her [2]________ she**'d left** the other sock.
***Yes/No* questions**	
'**Can** we have the parrot back?'	The Guatemalan family asked Darren if they **could** have the parrot back.
'**Have** you ever **cooked** anything before?'	Their Italian friends asked them [3]________ they**'d** ever **cooked** anything before.

1 **Complete the examples in the table above.**

9.07 2 **Put the words in the correct order to make sentences. Listen and check.**

1 the boy / had / his homework / done / the teacher / if / asked / he
The teacher asked the boy if he had done his homework.

2 doing / Laura / what / she / Jack / later / asked / was
____

3 me / ended / asked / my sister / how / the story / had
____

4 left / the assistant / any tickets / were / I / there / asked / if /
____

5 we / where / the station / an old man / was / asked
____

6 arrive / Tom / me / would / I / asked / what time
____

9.08 3 **Rewrite the sentences as reported questions. Listen and check.**

1 'Who's the hero of the story?' Mikhail asked his sister.
Mikhail asked his sister who the hero of the story was.

2 'Do you prefer comedy or drama?' Elena asked me.
____

3 Ruben asked his friend, 'Where did you hear that?'
____

4 'Will it rain later?' she asked.
____

5 'Can we still get tickets?' I asked the receptionist.
____

6 'What are you reading?' Sally asked me.
____

Use it!

4 **Think of five questions someone asked you last week. Write the names and tell your partner the questions. Can they guess who asked what?**

my maths teacher, my dad, my best friend Rachel, my sister, my cousin.

This person asked me if I had cleaned my room.

Your dad asked you if you had cleaned your room.

No, try again!

____

Finished? p126 Ex 3

SPEAKING

Telling an anecdote

9.09 **1 Look at the photo. What happened at the bowling alley? Listen to the conversation and check.**

9.09 **2 Complete the conversation with the phrases from the *Useful language* box. Listen and check.**

JAMIE [1] You'll never guess what happened to me last night.
ESMA No, what? Tell me.
JAMIE [2] ________ embarrassing! [3] ________ was, my new classmates asked me if I wanted to go bowling with them. I said yes and when we got there, they asked me how well I could bowl.
ESMA You didn't say you were any good, did you?
JAMIE Well, you know I'm a show-off! So I said, 'Just watch me!'
ESMA But you're terrible at bowling! I've seen you.
JAMIE Hey! I'm not that bad! So [4] ________, I picked up the ball, put my fingers in the holes, went to bowl …
ESMA Let me guess. Your fingers got stuck.
JAMIE Completely! I swung the ball back carefully and then swung it forward and just sort of went flying with it. The next [5] ________, I was flat on my back!
ESMA What a fantastic first impression!
JAMIE And to make matters worse, I couldn't get my fingers out.
ESMA Oh, Jamie!

Useful language

Basically, what happened was …
It was so (+ *adjective*)
So anyway, …
The next thing I knew …
You'll never guess what happened …

Watch video 9.4
Everyday English

Hey! Let me guess.
show-off sort of to make matters worse

3 Match the words in the *Everyday English* box with the words and phrases 1–5.

1 I disagree! ________
2 to make the situation even more unpleasant ________
3 someone who tries to make other people look at them ________
4 in a way ________
5 I think I know what you're going to say. ________

PLAN

4 Make notes on something embarrassing, funny, etc. that has happened to you.

Introduce the anecdote
Decide which details are the most important
End the anecdote

SPEAK

5 Practise telling the anecdote to your partner. Remember to use reported statements, commands and questions, vocabulary from this unit and phrases from the *Useful language* and *Everyday English* boxes.

CHECK

6 Work with another pair. Listen to their conversation and complete the notes.

What kind of anecdote was it? ________
____
What were the important details? ________
____
How did the anecdote end? ________
____

Free ice cream, anyone?

Most of us expect to receive presents on our birthday. However, Jimmy Teng or 'Uncle Jimmy' is different. The ice cream man from Singapore regularly gives away free ice cream on his birthday. He started the tradition on his 70th birthday when he offered to give away 700 free ice creams.

This year Uncle Jimmy announced that he was going to give away 1,000 free ice creams. Surprisingly, some customers insisted that they would pay for the ice cream. When asked why he did it, Mr Teng explained that nowadays everyone in Singapore was stressed and he wanted to make them feel happy. He also admitted that sharing ice cream made him feel good too. 'I'm so happy,' he said. 'I wouldn't be this happy if I won the lottery!'

Uncle Jimmy, who has been an ice cream man for over 15 years, has lots of customers. When asked what his favourite flavour was, he answered 'Sweetcorn' and he explained that ice cream in Singapore was sometimes served with bread rather than a cone.

WRITING

A news story

1 Why would someone give away free ice cream? Read the news story and check.

2 Read the news story again and answer the questions.

1 Who is the story about? ______
2 What happens? ______
3 When does it happen? ______

3 Discuss the questions about the structure of the story.

1 What does the headline tell us about the story? What doesn't it tell us?
2 What is the aim of the first sentence?
3 What do we learn in the first paragraph of the story?
4 When do we learn why the story happened?
5 Is the information in the third paragraph necessary or extra?
6 What effect does the direct speech have in the story?

4 Complete the phrases in the *Useful language* box with details from the news story.

Useful language

A man from [1] *Singapore regularly gives away free ice cream…*
He announced/explained/admitted that [2] ______
______
[3] '______,' he said.
Surprisingly/Nowadays etc., [4] ______
______
When asked … he answered/explained/said [5] ______
______

Write your own news story.

PLAN

5 Make notes on something special that someone has done to celebrate their birthday or find an interesting news story online.

WRITE

6 Write a news story about your idea in Exercise 5. Remember to include three paragraphs, language from this unit and phrases from the *Useful language* box.

CHECK

7 Do you …

- include an interesting headline?
- include some extra details in the third paragraph?
- include some direct speech?

Finished? p126 Ex 4

AROUND THE WORLD

Globetrotters

Watch video 9.5
Stories on stage

- Where do you think opera comes from? Where is it popular?
- What is *jingju* and what does it involve?
- What different skills do *jingju* performers need to have?

READING

A story

1 **Look at pictures A–D. What is happening in each one? Put them in order to make a story.**

2 (9.10) **Were your ideas correct? Read the introduction about Maori storytelling and the story 'How Maui slowed the Sun'.**

3 **Read the introduction and the story again. Write *T* (true) or *F* (false).**

1. The Maori have always written down their stories. F
2. It was impossible for the villagers to finish their work each day. ___
3. Maui had never done anything impressive before. ___
4. Only Maui's brothers helped to make the ropes. ___
5. The Sun saw Maui and his brothers coming closer. ___
6. Maui hit the Sun more than once with the bone. ___
7. The Sun stopped moving completely. ___

MAORI STORYTELLING

Storytelling is an essential part of the culture of the Maori people, the first inhabitants of Aotearoa (New Zealand). They didn't use to have a written language, so they learned stories by heart to remember their history. The Maori people still tell their stories, often in a traditional meeting place called a* marae*. The stories are accompanied by dance, songs and chants. Here is one for you to enjoy.

How Maui slowed the Sun

Long ago, the Sun used to move so quickly across the sky that the days were too short for people in the village to do all their work. The villager Maui, however, had a plan. He gathered his four brothers and said, 'Why should the Sun control us? Let's catch him and make him go more slowly.'

The brothers were worried. They asked Maui if it was really possible to get safely near the Sun. 'The heat and flames will burn us!' they said. 'We might die!' Maui held his grandfather's bone high, and said, 'I have achieved many things which you thought were impossible. I have brought fire to the people, I have caught the greatest fish in the world. With this bone, and with your help, I will catch the Sun.'

Everyone agreed to help him. Over the next five days they made strong ropes to catch the Sun. When they were ready, the brothers set off to the east, where the Sun rises. They travelled during the night so that the Sun wouldn't see them approaching. Eventually, they arrived at an enormous deep hole in the ground. This was where the Sun slept.

While the Sun was still asleep, the brothers built a wall around the hole and hid behind it, waiting patiently. Maui told his brothers not to throw the ropes until he said so. After a while, the ground began to shake. The Sun was waking up! First came his burning hair, then his fiery eyes and his white-hot teeth.

'Now!' cried Maui. The brothers threw the ropes over the Sun. They tangled in his hair and trapped his huge, hot body. The men pulled on the ropes as strongly as they could.

'What are you doing?' the Sun cried angrily.

Maui jumped on the wall and lifted up his grandfather's bone. He smashed it with all his strength down on the head of the Sun, who screamed in pain.

'Are you trying to kill me?'

'No, but you must go more slowly,' said Maui.

The Sun tried hard to escape, but again and again Maui hit him with the bone. The Sun gradually grew weaker, until at last he could only move slowly across the sky.

And that is why the days are now long enough for all our work, and why sometimes, if you look carefully, you can still see the ropes that connect the Sun to the Earth – shining through the clouds.

LEARN TO LEARN

Irregular adjective and noun pairs

Learn adjectives and their related nouns to increase your vocabulary.

4 **Complete the table with words from the story.**

Adjective	Noun
wide	width
1	height
hot	2
3	length
strong	4
5	depth

Summarising

Sometimes we need to tell a shorter version of a longer story. Summarising can help us to do this.

5 **Put the sentences in order to make a summary of the story.**

a The brothers travelled by night to where the Sun slept. ___
b You can still see the ropes that hold the Sun to the Earth. ___
c Maui hit the Sun with the bone. ___
d Maui, his brothers, and the villagers made strong ropes. ___
e People didn't use to have enough time to do everything because the Sun moved too quickly across the sky. 1
f The Sun eventually started to move more slowly. ___
g When the Sun woke up, the brothers trapped him. ___
h Maui had a plan to control the Sun. ___

Voice it!

6 **Discuss the questions.**

1 Without Maui, could the brothers have trapped the Sun?
2 Talk about a story from your culture. What does it mean?

Explore it!

Guess the correct answer.

Aotearoa, the Maori name for New Zealand, means land of …

a the perfect sky.
b the long white cloud.
c the towering mountains.

OWN IT! The Culture Project Teacher's Resource Bank

9 REVIEW

VOCABULARY

1 Match the reporting verbs in the box with the definitions.

admit	apologise	complain	deny	discover	promise

Which reporting verb do we use to …

1 say that something is not true? ________
2 tell someone you're sorry? ________
3 find out information for the first time? ________
4 agree that something is true? ________
5 tell someone formally something is wrong? ________
6 tell someone you will certainly do something? ________

2 Complete the sentences with the adverbs in the box.

eventually	fluently	gradually	nowadays	regularly	secretly	surprisingly

1 I ________ finished reading the book you recommended but it took me ages.
2 I speak French ________, mostly with my Canadian cousin – once a week.
3 Mike's family planned his birthday party ________. He was very surprised!
4 The exam was ________ easy. I finished it really quickly.
5 My best friend speaks English ________.
6 ________ I get on with my brother, but we didn't use to.
7 My English is improving ________ but I need to learn more vocabulary.

LANGUAGE IN ACTION

3 Complete the second sentences.

1 'I'll help you with your homework.'
Ayaz offered ________
2 'Send me a message when you get there.'
Shaun told me ________
3 'Why don't we meet at the new café?'
Ada suggested ________
4 'I promise I'll give you a lift.'
She promised ________

4 Rewrite the direct questions as reported questions.

1 'Do you often read the news online?' my sister asked me.
____
____
2 'How can I improve my English?' Zehra asked her teacher.
____
____
3 'Have you seen what's happened in London?' Ian asked Jake.
____
____
4 'Will the museum be open tomorrow?' the tourist asked.
____
____

Self-assessment

I can use reporting verbs.

I can use adverbs of time and manner.

I can use reported statements and commands.

I can use reported questions.

LEARN TO ... ASK FOR HELP WHEN YOU DON'T UNDERSTAND

There are different ways to ask English speakers for help and check you understand what they've said.

1 Read the problems people have understanding someone in English. Then discuss the questions.

We asked six language learners what problems they'd had understanding people in English. This is what they told us.

1 For me, it's usually that the other person speaks too fast.

2 The worst thing is when people use lots of difficult words I don't know

3 I usually understand more or less, but I don't understand all of the details.

4 Sometimes I think I've understood someone, but then I realise I haven't at all!

5 My problem is that when I don't understand I'm too shy to say. I just say 'yes' a lot!

Have you had any of these problems? How did you solve them?

2 Read the conversations. Match phrases 1–5 with phrases with similar meanings a–e.

a Could you repeat from the beginning? ___
b I want to make sure I've understood correctly. ___
c What's the meaning of that word? ___
d I didn't hear the last thing you said. ___
e What were your instructions? ___

1
BEN Sorry, Miss. I didn't understand. [1]**What did you say I had to do?**
TEACHER I told you to compare the two pictures and discuss how similar they are.
BEN [2]**What does 'similar' mean?**

2
ALISON Excuse me, can you tell me how to get to the post office, please?
MAN IN Sure. Go straight until you see a big building. It's opposite that …
ALISON [3]**I didn't catch that.** The big what?
MAN IN Building.

3
GISELLE Bea thought Juan had promised he would bring the food, but he hadn't! After a while, someone said-
JO Wait, wait, wait! [4]**Can you start again, please?** I'm lost!
GISELLE Sorry, sorry. What happened was that …

4
VLAD Which bus do I need for Oxford Park?
WOMAN You need two, actually. Take the 147 fromhere to Austen Square, cross the road and then take the 29 from in front of the bank.
VLAD OK, [5]**let me check I've got this right.** First, I take 147 to Austen Square?
WOMAN That's right.

OWN IT!

3 Student A: choose one of the topics in the box and explain it to Student B. Student B: use the phrases from the conversations in Exercise 2 to help you understand. Then swap roles.

how to get from your school to your house the story of how Maui slowed the Sun the rules of a sport

5 FINISHED?

1 Put the letters in order to write two verbs to describe processes.

1 eodseaptwlev *develop waste*
2 uclertoplocced ___________
3 evaemrrilusede ___________
4 lepmtapmnicocsuyu ___________
5 toeercaslev ___________
6 toctacrenactnt ___________

2 Mark is going to have an operation next week. Complete the sentences about who will be doing what. Put the sentences in order.

a Next, the anaesthetic ___________ (give) by Dr Sanna. ☐
b The second part of the operation ___________ (do) by Dr Rees. ☐
c At first, his heart rate ___________ (measure) by Nurse Evans. ☐
d Finally, he ________ (take) home by Nurse Simms. ☐
e Until he is completely better, he ___________ (visit) in hospital by Dr Jones. ☐
f The first part of the operation ___________ (do) by Dr Lansbury. ☐

3 How many sentences can you write that go in front of these question tags in three minutes?

1 …, isn't it?
It's freezing today
2 …, doesn't she?
____
3 …, can't they?
____
4 …, would you?
____
5 …, are we?
____
6 …, haven't you?
____
7 …, had he?
____

4 Circle nine more extreme adjectives.

F	E	T	D	E	A	F	E	N	I	N	G
R	A	N	E	E	F	R	L	J	A	B	P
E	H	S	O	R	A	F	L	Q	M	O	U
E	D	S	C	R	R	U	I	J	Q	I	N
Z	R	W	T	I	M	I	A	U	J	L	D
I	E	J	J	U	N	O	F	F	I	I	Q
N	A	V	X	X	N	A	U	Y	R	N	B
G	D	V	F	Y	O	N	T	S	I	G	V
D	F	F	C	S	W	I	I	I	K	N	A
B	U	M	L	R	X	N	X	N	N	E	G
V	L	M	A	T	B	T	E	C	G	G	H
M	A	R	V	E	L	L	O	U	S	Z	D
A	B	L	Z	G	O	R	G	E	O	U	S

6 FINISHED?

1 **Read the clues and complete the crossword.**

Across

2 I always have … with my friends.
5 I get a lot … of my English lessons.
7 We switched off the TV because we got … with the programme.
9 Do you take an … in football?
11 My dad always gets … when he's driving.
12 My grandfather never had the … to go to university.

Down

1 We have 30 minutes before our train arrives, so let's take … of it.
3 My annoying cousin really gets on my … .
4 I have … about whether my team will win tomorrow.
6 My grandmother takes a lot of … in looking at old photos.
8 It's important to take some … in life.
10 I got to … a lot of new people at summer camp last year.

2 **Match the jokes with the answers.**
Give each joke a score (one star = terrible, five stars = very funny).

1 If you dialled 08968 767 457 454 233 989 767 521 123, what would you get? ___
2 What would happen if you put your music in the fridge? ___
3 What word would become shorter if you added two more letters to it? ___
4 Where would a cow go if it wanted a holiday? ___
5 If you look in any dictionary, which word will always be spelled wrong? ___

a Mooooo York! ★★★★★

b A very tired finger! ☆☆☆☆☆

c Wrong. ★★★★★

d Short! ☆☆☆☆☆

e You'd get some really cool music! ★★★★★

3 **Complete the sentences with third conditional verbs and interesting information to continue the story.**

1 If Sara hadn't gone to school that day, she wouldn't have met ________.
2 If she hadn't met ________ she wouldn't have found out ________.
3 If she hadn't ________________________.
4 If ____________________________.
5 If ____________________________.

4 **Put the letters in order to make verbs and nouns for inspiration and challenge.**

1 a c e e g h l l n *challenge*
2 y e b r a r v ________
3 d t r i a i n o t n m e e ________
4 o p r u i y t n t o p ________
5 b t c e l a s o ________
6 u p r t o p s ________
7 n o r g e a u c e ________
8 o e c m v r o e ________
9 a e c v h e i ________
10 e i n r i s p ________

7 FINISHED?

1 Find the letters and then write them to make the first half of a message. Can you guess the second half?

1 satisfied (letter 2)
2 hopeful (letter 1)
3 peaceful (letter 5)
4 eager (letter 2)
5 glad (letter 2)
6 hurt (letter 4)
7 thrilled (letter 2)
8 annoyed (letter 5)
9 amused (letter 2)
10 ridiculous (letter 4)
11 insecure (letter 2)
12 down (letter 1)

a h _ _ _ _ _ _ _ _ _ _ _ is as important as
a _ _ _ _ _ _ _ _ _ _ _ _ .

2 Four brothers each have a sister who is the complete opposite of them. Match the sentences halves to find out who the sisters are.

Jack keeps eating chocolate all day
Emily avoids eating too much sugar.

Alex never stops	getting up early.
Berat hopes	eating chocolate all day.
Charlie always forgets	to stay in the city forever.
Jacob doesn't mind	talking in class.
Jack keeps	to put his notebook in his bag.

Emily avoids	to get up late every day if she could.
Sara always remembers	to speak during most lessons.
Megan refuses	living in the countryside.
Olivia would love	to take all her books to class.
Mira misses	eating too much sugar.

3 How many pairs of subject and object questions can you write in three minutes using the ideas in the box?

Q: What did Al Zahrawi write?
A: One of the earliest books about medicine.
Q: Who wrote one of the earliest books about medicine?
A: Al Zahrawi.

write
invent
J.K. Rowling
the Ancient Egyptians
build
the iPhone
Steve Jobs
discover
one of the earliest books about medicine
the Italians
gravity
the Pyramids
Isaac Newton
the iPod
the Harry Potter stories
the Pyramids
pizza
Al Zahrawi

4 Put the letters in order and add *heart* or *mind* to make an expression.

yellow: *put my (heart) into*
blue: ______
red: ______
brown: ______
pink: ______
orange: ______
purple: ______
green: ______

	M	T	P	I	T
G	E	U	O	Y	N
S	D	O	L	N	Y
C	H	C	E	E	H
I	S	Y	O	C	M
Y	O	S	M	G	A
S	N	T	N	B	Y
R	O	R	E	L	A
M	T	N	S	R	B
E	I	W	A	O	E
M	E	N	E	'	B
O	A	B	S	M	K
T	I	R	D	O	Y

8 FINISHED?

1 Use the code to complete the questions. Answer them so they are true for you.

A	B	C	D	E	F	G	H	I	J	K	L	M	N	O	P	Q	R	S	T	U	V	W	X	Y	Z
8		24	11	19			12	14		22	17			18			2	26	13	21	6	10		4	

1 W H I C H   A D V E R T S   D O   Y O U   L I K E ?
10 12 14 24 12   8 11 6 19 2 13 26   11 18   4 18 21   17 14 22 19

2 W _ _ C _   L O _ O _   _ O   _ O _   _ _ O W ?
10 12 14 24 12   17 18 25 18 26   11 18   4 18 21   22 1 18 10

3 _ O   _ O _   E V E _   W _ _ T E   _ E V _ E W _ ?
11 18   4 18 21   19 6 19 2   10 2 14 13 19   2 19 6 14 19 10 26

4 _ O   _ O _   _ _ E   A _   _ L O C _ E _ _ ?
11 18   4 18 21   21 26 19   8 11   15 17 18 24 22 19 2 26

5 W _ A T   _ _ _ L _ E _ C E _   _ O _   T O   _ _ _   A   _ _ O _ _ C T ?
10 12 8 13   14 1 20 17 21 19 1 24 19 26   4 18 21   13 18   15 21 4   8   23 2 18 11 21 24 13

6 W _ _ C _   _ L O _ A _ _   C A _   _ O _   _ E _ E _ _ E _ ?
10 12 14 24 12   26 17 18 25 8 1 26   24 8 1   4 18 21   2 19 16 19 16 15 19 2

2 Complete the sentences with a relative pronoun. Guess what each thing or person is. Use the scrambled words in the box to help you.

1 It's a feeling you have ________ someone has helped you. ________
2 It's a word ________ goes with *have* and means 'a good time'. ________
3 It describes a place ________ you can feel very calm and relaxed. ________
4 It's a word ________ means 'very interesting'. ________
5 It describes someone ________ feels quite angry. ________
6 It's someone ________ products are bought by someone else. ________

lgruafte unf lpeuafce fganisctian daneyon relsler

3 Circle five pronouns in the wordsnake. Use them to complete the sentences so they are true for you.

temyselfonboanyonesetsomeoneoranysomethingeverynothingeach

The last time I …

1 enjoyed ________ was ________________
________________________________.
2 didn't talk to ________ for an hour was ______
________________________________.
3 helped ________ was ________________
________________________________.
4 forgot ________ important was ____________
________________________________.
5 had ________ to eat and felt hungry was _____
________________________________.

4 Circle nine more Internet verbs.

K	W	G	B	I	C	B	K	A	A	N	N	P
S	H	U	T	D	O	W	N	Y	V	K	O	I
O	T	E	B	I	R	C	S	B	U	S	T	W
G	Y	F	S	B	D	R	M	U	N	F	N	O
G	O	N	F	E	U	T	S	O	P	O	E	Q
J	Z	L	L	O	A	I	H	Y	D	L	M	Y
W	S	E	V	E	H	C	L	E	M	L	M	E
Y	T	H	X	X	T	C	H	D	Y	O	O	Y
E	U	S	R	I	X	Q	T	C	U	W	C	Y
E	X	N	W	N	H	L	M	I	Z	P	E	A
E	S	S	T	N	I	R	P	R	W	X	D	B
D	H	X	K	Q	S	H	K	H	X	S	G	C
P	Y	P	W	C	K	R	O	S	U	B	C	F

9 FINISHED?

1 **Match the squares to make reporting verbs.**

de | apolo | ann | con | com | ad | in | sug | re | pro

plain | mise | ny | ounce | gest | sist | mit | fuse | firm | gise

2 **Write examples of the following.**

A time when you …

1 suggested doing something different. ______
2 offered to help someone. ______
3 denied that you had done something and then admitted that you had done it. ______
4 promised to do something. ______
5 insisted that you did something. ______
6 told someone to do something. ______

3 **Imagine you are a famous athlete, pop star or actor. How many things can you list that you've often been asked by fans in three minutes?**

Lionel Messi
My fans have often asked me …
… what my dream team would be.
… if I get nervous before taking a penalty.
______
______
______
______
______

4 **Complete the sentences with the adverbs in the box. What is the adverb in the boxed letters?**

after a while | eventually | fluently | gradually | ~~nowadays~~ | patiently | regularly | secretly | surprisingly

1 Most people *n* [*o*] *w a d a y s* have a mobile.
2 I whispered _ _ [*c*] _ _ _ _ _ to her.
[*c*]
3 _ _ _ _ _ [ ] _ _ _ _ _, the baby fell asleep.
4 The twins are _ _ _ _ _ _ [ ] _ _ _ _ _ different.
5 The teacher waited _ _ _ [ ] _ _ _ _ _ _.
[*o*]
[*n*]
6 The rain _ _ _ _ _ _ _ [ ] _ _ _ stopped.
7 Aroha spoke Maori _ [ ] _ _ _ _ _ _ _.
8 English gets _ _ _ _ _ _ _ [ ] _ _ easier.
9 The Olympics take place _ _ _ _ _ _ _ _ _ [ ].

5 VOCABULARY BANK

Processes

attract collect	communicate connect	create deliver	develop measure	produce solve	supply waste

1 Match 1–5 with a–e.

1 The parcel was delivered ________
2 This course will help you to develop ________
3 The new factory will create ________
4 I need to collect ________
5 We hope the museum will attract ________

a hundreds of jobs.
b to the wrong house.
c more tourists to the area.
d some books from the library.
e your communication skills.

Extreme adjectives

boiling

deafening

dreadful

enormous

fascinating

freezing

gorgeous

marvellous

stunning

terrifying

2 Put the letters in order to make extreme adjectives.

1 Before the electricity was connected, our house was *engefzir* in winter. ________
2 The crowd produced a *engafedni* noise. ________
3 They measured the bones and discovered that the creature was *eomosurn*. ________
4 It's *dafreuld* to waste so much water. ________
5 She's able to communicate difficult ideas in a *nafsatingci* way. ________

LEARN TO LEARN

Personalising new vocabulary

Using personalised sentences helps you to remember new vocabulary.

3 Choose four words from the list above and use them to write questions to ask your partner.

1 ________________________________
2 ________________________________
3 ________________________________
4 ________________________________

What is the most fascinating book you've ever read? *Treasure Island*

6 VOCABULARY BANK

Verb collocations with *get*, *take* and *have*

get a lot out of	get on my nerves	have fun	take an interest in
get bored	get to know	have the chance	take pleasure in
get lost	have doubts	take advantage of	take risks

1 Put the words in the correct order to make sentences.

1 better / know / to / I'd / her / get / like / to / . I think she's very interesting.

____

2 lot / Simon / course / got / a / of / the / out / . He said it was very useful.

____

3 the / at / picnic / you / did / fun / have / ? You certainly had good weather for it.

____

4 get / some / nerves / of / on / my / my / classmates / . They're quite annoying.

____

Inspiration and challenge

bravery (n)

challenge (n)

determination (n)

obstacle (n)

opportunity (n)

achieve (v)

encourage (v)

inspire (v)

overcome (v)

support (v)

2 Underline the incorrect words in each sentence.

1 Harry managed to overcome the *problem* / *solution* / *obstacle*.

2 Mrs Betts always tries to encourage her *students* / *children* / *happiness*.

3 Luke has the determination to achieve his *salary* / *goals* / *ambition*.

4 I think we were all inspired by her *speech* / *bravery* / *disappointment*.

LEARN TO LEARN

Stress patterns

Knowing the stress pattern of a word can help you pronounce it and hear it when people say it.

3 Write the stress pattern for each word. The first one has been done for you.

1 bravery *Ooo* 2 encourage ______ 3 opportunity ______

7 VOCABULARY BANK

Feelings

amused

annoyed

down

eager

glad

grateful

hopeful

hurt

insecure

peaceful

ridiculous

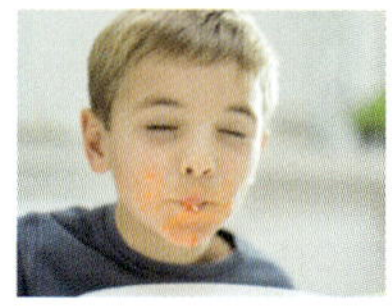
satisfied

thrilled

1 Complete the statements with the words in the box. Do you agree or disagree?

eager grateful insecure peaceful ridiculous

	Agree	Not sure	Disagree
1 I feel ________ when friends remember my birthday.	☐	☐	☐
2 I feel a bit ________ about the future.	☐	☐	☐
3 I feel ________ in a hat.	☐	☐	☐
4 I am always ________ to try new experiences.	☐	☐	☐
5 I feel ________ when I am in the countryside.	☐	☐	☐

Expressions with *heart* and *mind*

be in two minds
bear in mind
break someone's heart
change your mind
close to your heart
cross your mind
have something on your mind
learn by heart
make your mind up
put your heart into something

2 Circle the correct words.

1 Leaving my girlfriend behind in Australia *was close to my heart / broke my heart / changed my mind.*
2 I'm annoyed because you won't *make your mind up / learn by heart / cross your mind* about the party.
3 Winning was important to Max and he really *had it on his mind / bore it in mind / put his heart into it.*
4 I'm *in two minds / crossing my mind / bearing in mind* about telling my sister the truth.

LEARN TO LEARN

Gapped flashcards

Using gapped flashcards can help you learn expressions.

3 Use the flashcards you made in class. Take turns to pick up a flashcard, look at the front and make a sentence. Score two points for a correct sentence but lose a point if you look at the back.

*I was going to go swimming but I **changed my mind**.*

8 VOCABULARY BANK

Advertising

ad blocker	brand	logo	review
advert	buyer	marketing company	seller
advertise	influence	product	slogan

1 Complete the sentences with a noun from the same word family as the verb.

1 They're looking for someone to buy their company. They want a ________ .
2 Dan reviews hotels online. He writes ________ .
3 They advertise on the London Underground. They have ________ there.
4 She has a factory that produces mugs. Its ________ is mugs.
5 I'm not influenced by celebrity vloggers. They don't have any ________ on me.

Internet verbs

build up	delete	post	subscribe	switch on
comment on	follow	shut down	switch off	vlog

2 Use verbs from the list above to complete the questions. Ask and answer them.

1 Do you ________ anyone online?
2 What would influence you to ________ to an online magazine?
3 What subject does your favourite YouTuber ________ about?
4 Would you ________ an online comment if it upset a friend?
5 Do you ever ________ other people's posts?

LEARN TO LEARN

Collocations

When you learn a new verb, try to learn the nouns that go with it. This will help your English sound natural.

3 Match the verb 1–5 with its noun collocation a–e. Can you think of any other nouns that go with these verbs?

1 shut down	a followers
2 follow	b a post
3 build up	c a phone
4 switch off	d a vlogger
5 comment on	e an account

9 VOCABULARY BANK

Reporting verbs

admit announce	apologise claim	complain confirm	deny discover	insist promise	refuse suggest

1 Complete the sentences with the correct form of a reporting verb from the list above.

1 'I stole the money.' She ________ that she had stolen the money.
2 'The hotel was really dirty.' My mother ________ about the hotel.
3 'I'll definitely be back by nine o'clock.' Samantha ________ that she would be back by nine o'clock.
4 'I'm certainly not going to help.' Adam ________ to help us.
5 'I'm so sorry that I lied to you.' Tom ________ for lying.

Adverbs of time and manner

after a while eventually	fluently gradually	nowadays occasionally	patiently regularly	secretly surprisingly

2 Circle the correct words.

1 They waited *secretly / patiently / gradually* for Max to arrive.
2 It was raining for hours but *eventually / regularly / nowadays* it stopped.
3 The food in the restaurant was *fluently / secretly / surprisingly* nice.
4 At first I found the lessons difficult, but *occasionally / after a while / regularly* I got better at them.
5 I went running every day and *fluently / patiently / gradually* I got fitter.

LEARN TO LEARN

Recording words in sentences

Writing down new words in a sentence helps you to remember them.

3 Choose four words from the list above and write sentences that are true for you. Then tell your partner.

1 ____________________
2 ____________________
3 ____________________
4 ____________________

I usually drink coffee but occasionally I drink tea.

6 CITIZENSHIP

1 Discuss the questions.

1. What is digital citizenship?
2. How can the way we use technology affect our relationships with people?

2 6.12 **Read the article. Check your answers to Exercise 1.**

3 Read the nine themes of digital citizenship and mark (✓) the ones that apply to each case study. Some apply to both and some to neither.

Nine Themes of Digital Citizenship	CS1	CS2
1 Have equal access to technology.	✗	✗
2 Buy and sell safely online.		
3 Share information safely.		
4 Learn how to use technology appropriately.		
5 Follow an ethical code of conduct.		
6 Use technology lawfully.		
7 Act responsibly.		
8 Promote physical and psychological well-being.		
9 Protect online safety.		

4 Discuss the questions in the case studies in the article.

5 Complete the sentences with the words in bold in the article.

1. That is a very ________ photo. You look great!
2. You cannot ________ some websites to be safe. You should check your online privacy.
3. Please don't ________ me. Turn off your phone and listen to what I am saying.
4. I am going to ________ how often I use social media. I want to use it less.
5. He is always very polite and ________ when he sends messages.

Digital citizenship: case studies

Today's citizens can make the most of living, learning, and working in a digital world. However, this brings responsibilities as well as opportunities, as these digital citizens need to act in a safe, legal, and ethical way. Digital citizenship is similar to traditional citizenship in that it means being kind, **respectful** and ready to take part in activities that make the world a better place.

If teens take risks with the way they use digital devices, it could lead to problems. These case studies illustrate some common situations.

Case study 1

Some friends are having fun at the beach. Later, one of them posts photos of the others online. She does not ask permission and some of the pictures are not very **flattering**. If you had been in possession of these pictures, what would you have done?

Case study 2

A group of friends are sitting in a café. One of them gets a call on his phone. He answers the call, **ignores** his friends, and has a loud, personal conversation in front of them. How would you feel if you were in the group?

The way these people use technology raises serious questions about **trust**, friendship and social relationships.

Digital citizenship involves many things, from sharing information safely to acting responsibly online. If we want to get the best out of a fast-changing world, we should **monitor** our digital habits. In this way we can meet the challenge of becoming good digital citizens.

Explore it!

Guess the correct answer.

In an average lifetime, people will spend … on social media.

a one year and two months
b three years and five months
c five years and four months

Find another interesting fact about the digital world. Write a question for your partner to answer.

8 ART AND DESIGN

1 **Discuss the questions.**

1. Where do you see print adverts?
2. How do print adverts communicate their messages?
3. What are the main elements of a print advert?

8.11 2 **Read the article. Check your answers to Exercise 1.**

How to design an effective print advert

We are surrounded by print adverts. When we walk down the street, there are slogans, logos and images everywhere. Think about how many adverts you have seen today. How many of them can you actually remember?

Marketing companies, which are responsible for advertising campaigns, charge a lot of money for their services. Therefore, a printed message needs to effectively communicate a brand's image. In fact, the person who creates an advert is a communicator more than a designer. So how is an **effective** print advert designed?

The **headline** is the most important element. An advert has approximately two seconds to catch the reader's eye, so the headline needs to be clear and focus on one idea. A **subhead**, which still needs to be brief, can then give more information.

Next is the image. Sometimes an image can become the centre of attention and distract from the message of a print advert. The headline and image need to work well together and it is essential that the image is relevant to the product. Also, advertising research shows men and women respond to images differently. Many advertisers use brighter colours in adverts for women and darker shapes in adverts for men.

Once an advert has these features, it is time to decide on a final **layout**. The top-to-bottom layout in the picture, which is widely used, is very effective. Most adverts influence potential buyers with the most important information at the top.

A good advert tells us we need things that previously we didn't even know existed. Next time you walk down a street full of print adverts, think about how effective they are.

3 **Complete the sentences with your own ideas.**

1. Marketing companies need to effectively communicate a brand's image because …
2. A headline is the most important element of a print advert because …
3. An image should not be the main focus of a print advert because …
4. Different images are used for men and women in print adverts because …

4 **Choose an idea and turn it into a headline of three or four words for an advert.**

1. This toothpaste will leave your mouth fresh and clean and your teeth white.
2. You must buy these jeans because they are more comfortable and cheaper than others.

____

____

5 **Complete the definitions with the words in bold in the article.**

1. ________ (n) the design of something
2. ________ (n) the title written in big letters
3. ________ (n) heading that comes after the headline
4. ________ (adj) successful

Explore it!

Guess the correct answer.

More than … a year is spent on advertising.

a $6 billion b $60 billion c $600 billion

Find another interesting fact about advertising. Write a question for your partner to answer.

UNIT 5

The letters *mb* and *bt*

5.07 **1 Listen and repeat.**

1 She's a climber. 2 I doubt he's coming.

2 Circle the silent *b* in each sentence.

1 I saw a film about a bomb.
2 I haven't got any debts.
3 He hurt his thumb with a hammer.
4 I saw a sheep with two lambs.

5.08 **3 Listen, check and repeat.**

UNIT 6

Stress in multi-syllable words

6.02 **1 Listen and repeat.**

1 temperature 2 different 3 comfortable

6.03 **2 Underline the stressed syllable in each word. Listen and check.**

1 interesting 4 category 7 vegetable
2 Wednesday 5 chocolate 8 memorable
3 business 6 secondary

3 Identify the syllables which are not pronounced.

1 interesting

4 Practise saying the words in Exercise 2.

UNIT 7

Initial consonant clusters with *s*

7.07 **1 Listen and repeat.**

1 stress 3 strength
2 strong 4 straight

7.08 **2 Listen and repeat the tongue-twisters.**

1 **Strong** winds **spread** the sparks through the **streets**.
2 Stella's got **straight** hair and **stripes** on her skirt.
3 Stuart **sprayed** his phone with a **screen** cleaner.

7.09 **3 Listen, repeat and practise the words.**

UNIT 8

The letters *-tion*

8.04 **1 Listen and repeat.**

1 /ʃən/ celebration 2 /tʃən/ suggestion

2 Look at the *-tion* ending in the words. Write *1* (/ʃən/) or *2* (/tʃən/).

1 position 1 5 connection ___
2 digestion ___ 6 question ___
3 contribution ___ 7 indigestion ___
4 vacation ___

8.05 **3 Listen, check and repeat.**

4 Answer the questions.

1 What's your idea of the perfect celebration?
2 What question would you like to ask your favourite celebrity?
3 Where would you go for your ideal vacation?

UNIT 9

The letters *cia*

9.02 **1 Listen and repeat.**

1 social 3 musician 5 commercial
2 sociable 4 special

2 Practise saying the words.

1 magician 4 politician
2 beneficial 5 mathematician
3 artificial

9.03 **3 Listen, check and repeat.**

4 Student A reads a definition. Student B says the correct word from Exercises 1 or 2.

1 When someone likes meeting new people.
2 Someone who likes numbers.
3 Something good and useful.
4 Someone who plays an instrument.
5 Not real or natural.
6 Someone who takes a rabbit out of a hat.

IRREGULAR VERBS

Infinitive	Past simple	Past participle
be	was/were	been
beat	beat	beaten
become	became	become
begin	began	begun
bite	bit	bitten
blow	blew	blown
break	broke	broken
bring	brought	brought
build	built	built
buy	bought	bought
catch	caught	caught
choose	chose	chosen
come	came	come
cost	cost	cost
cut	cut	cut
do	did	done
draw	drew	drawn
drink	drank	drunk
drive	drove	driven
eat	ate	eaten
fall	fell	fallen
feel	felt	felt
fight	fought	fought
find	found	found
fly	flew	flown
forget	forgot	forgotten
get	got	got
give	gave	given
go	went	gone
grow	grew	grown
hang	hung	hung
have	had	had
hear	heard	heard
hide	hid	hidden
hit	hit	hit
hold	held	held
hurt	hurt	hurt
keep	kept	kept
know	knew	known
leave	left	left
lend	lent	lent

Infinitive	Past simple	Past participle
let	let	let
lie	lied	lied
light	lit	lit
lose	lost	lost
make	made	made
mean	meant	meant
meet	met	met
pay	paid	paid
put	put	put
read	read	read
ride	rode	ridden
ring	rang	rung
rise	rose	risen
run	ran	run
say	said	said
see	saw	seen
sell	sold	sold
send	sent	sent
shine	shone	shone
shoot	shot	shot
show	showed	shown
shut	shut	shut
sing	sang	sung
sit	sat	sat
sleep	slept	slept
speak	spoke	spoken
spend	spent	spent
stand	stood	stood
steal	stole	stolen
swim	swam	swum
take	took	taken
teach	taught	taught
tear	tore	torn
tell	told	told
think	thought	thought
throw	threw	thrown
understand	understood	understood
wake	woke	woken
wear	wore	worn
win	won	won
write	wrote	written

OWN IT! 4

B1 Preliminary test content in *Own It!* Level 4 has been checked by Cambridge Assessment English for accuracy and level.

WORKBOOK

Eoin Higgins and Philip Wood

CAMBRIDGE UNIVERSITY PRESS

CONTENTS

Unit 5 Wonderful world p40

Unit 6 No limits p48

Unit 7 Keep calm! p56

Unit 8 Advertising p64

Unit 9 Have you heard the news? p72

Exam tips and practice p80

Language reference and practice p96

Language bank p108

Irregular verbs p111

5 WONDERFUL WORLD

VOCABULARY

Processes

1 ★ Find 11 more verbs in the word search. Write them below. You have the first letter of each verb.

C	O	(P	R	O	D	U	C	E)	P	Z	C
M	E	A	S	U	R	E	G	V	C	Q	O
E	S	C	S	U	P	P	L	Y	R	M	M
B	R	T	I	D	E	L	I	V	E	R	M
Z	A	R	O	E	Y	U	I	D	A	C	U
N	S	I	C	V	C	O	L	E	T	O	N
C	O	N	N	E	C	T	O	P	E	L	I
H	L	O	T	L	O	I	L	L	O	L	C
T	V	P	G	O	L	B	N	Z	G	E	A
E	E	X	V	P	A	T	T	R	A	C	T
W	Y	G	I	U	V	K	W	A	S	T	E

1 p *roduce*
2 m ________
3 s ________
4 d ________
5 c ________
6 a ________
7 w ________
8 c ________
9 c ________
10 d ________
11 c ________
12 s ________

2 ★★ Circle the correct options. (see the *Learn to learn* tip in the Student's Book, p59.)

1 The school supplied us ________ books and other materials for the project.
   a with   b for   c on

2 Flowers attract bees and other insects ________ bright colours and nice smells.
   a about   b with   c at

3 We measured the distance ________ the door to the window.
   a between   b with   c from

3 ★★ Complete the amazing facts with verbs from Exercise 1.

1 The albatross, a type of seabird, has wings that *measure* almost 3.5 metres.

2 Some scientists say that trees in forests ________ with each other.

3 One cow can ________ around 12 litres of milk every day.

4 Europeans ________ an average of around 180 kilograms of food every year.

5 The man who ________ pizza to the 2014 Oscars ceremony got a tip of $1,000 from the actors.

6 The UK tea company Twinings have been ________ the British Royal family with tea since 1837.

4 ★★★ Find out some other amazing facts and write sentences about them. Use verbs from Exercise 1.

The tallest building in the world is the Burj Khalifa in Dubai. It measures 828 metres.

____

____

Explore it!

Guess the correct answer.

True or false? Cats always land on their feet.

Find out a fact about an animal and write a true/false sentence about it.

- Write it on a piece of paper.
- Stick it to the wall in your classroom.
- Ask your classmates to choose the correct answer.
- Count how many students choose the correct answer.

READING

A webzine article

1 ★ **Read the article quickly. What colour is the Aurora Borealis normally? In what colour has it been seen in the south of Europe?**

2 ★★ **Match the underlined words in the article with the definitions 1–6.**

1. when the sun appears in the sky _sunrise_
2. used physical force to win against someone ________
3. spirits of dead people ________
4. problems or difficulties ________
5. parts of a war, fights between two armies ________
6. the person who makes something ________

3 ★★ **Read the article again. Are the sentences *T* (true) or *F* (false)? Correct the false sentences.**

1. Aurora, Helios and Selene were all sisters.
   F Helios was the brother of Aurora and Selene.
2. It is unusual to find stories about the Aurora Borealis in different cultures.
   ____
3. The French Revolution happened after red lights were seen in the sky over England and Scotland.
   ____
4. The Cree Indians in Canada believed the lights were a bad sign.
   ____
5. The Vikings believed the lights helped dead soldiers to their resting place.
   ____
6. Electrical energy from the sun produces the Aurora Borealis.
   ____

4 ★★★ **Write your answer to the question at the end of the article.**

____

____

Aurora Borealis: A wonder of nature

Origin of the name

The Aurora Borealis is an amazing natural light show around the Arctic Circle – a wonder of nature. The name comes from Ancient Greek – *aurora* meaning 'sunrise' and *boreas* meaning 'wind'. The Ancient Greeks believed that Aurora was the sister of Helios (the sun god) and Selene (the moon goddess). As the sun rose in the morning, Aurora flew across the sky to remind her brother and sister that a new day had arrived. Strange stories connected to the lights are found in many cultures.

Europe: bad signs

It was strange that the lights, normally green in colour, were seen in Greece. Scientists believe that the lights appeared red so far south. In 1789, red lights were seen by the inhabitants of England and Scotland. Shortly after this the French Revolution started, and many believed that the lights had been a sign of the trouble to come.

North America: other meanings

The Algonquin Indians in Canada believed the lights came from a fire that was built by Nanahbozah, their creator. This fire was a sign that Nanahbozah was watching over everyone. Their neighbours, the Cree Indians, on the other hand, thought that the lights were like ghosts who were trying to communicate with the living.

Viking women

Another ancient civilization – the Vikings – thought the lights were made by the Valkyrie, women who fought in their battles. This light delivered dead soldiers safely to Valhalla, where they could finally rest.

The scientific explanation

Now we know that the lights are created by the sun. Sometimes, scientists say, the sun sends huge amounts of electrical energy into space. When this energy reaches Earth, it produces these strange lights in the sky. … But which explanation do you prefer?

LANGUAGE IN ACTION

The passive

1 ☆ **Circle the correct options.**

1. This coffee (is) / *are* produced in Kenya – try it.
2. The problem with my computer *was* / *were* solved by switching it off and then on again.
3. In the future, lots of diseases *are* / *will be* cured with technology.
4. We're going to recycle all the plastic bags so nothing will be *waste* / *wasted*.
5. Some people thought the Aurora Borealis *is* / *was* created by gods.
6. Was there a loud bang when all the cables *was* / *were* connected?

2 ☆☆ **Complete the sentences with the correct form of the verbs in the box.**

attract	build	collect	~~deliver~~	measure	use

1. These books ___*will be delivered*___ tomorrow morning to your house.
2. The church ____________ in the 15th century, but now it's a library.
3. Huge rocks ____________ to build Stonehenge in England.
4. The ingredients ____________ carefully, but the cake still tasted strange.
5. Old clothes ____________ at the school, and we'll give them all away to charity.
6. The picnic is terrible! These flies ____________ to the food. They're everywhere!

3 ☆☆ **Complete the conversation with the correct form of the verbs in brackets.**

CHRIS Hey Alison, let's see if you can answer these questions.

ALISON A quiz? OK.

CHRIS Right, first question. How many languages [1] ___*are spoken*___ (speak) in India?

ALISON Em … it's a lot, I know that. 200?

CHRIS No, 400! Next one: When [2] ____________ the first mobile phone app ____________ (create)?

ALISON I think it was 1998.

CHRIS Very good! What [3] ____________ (measure) in megabits per second?

ALISON That's easy! Your internet connection speed.

CHRIS And … where [4] ____________ 5.6 million cars ____________ (produce) in 2017?

ALISON Em … France?

CHRIS No, it was in Germany. So, after all your hard work, would you like a pizza?

ALISON Great idea. But first answer this question. What [5] ____________ (deliver) by drones in the future?

CHRIS That's obvious … PIZZA!!

4 ☆☆☆ **Write five passive sentences about mobile phones. Use these ideas.**

1. What are they made of?
2. Where are they produced?
3. What year was an important model produced?
4. How are apps downloaded?
5. How will they be used in the future?

____

____

____

____

____

VOCABULARY AND LISTENING

Extreme adjectives

1 ☆ **Circle the correct options.**

We visited New York in January. It's a [1]*stunning / dreadful* city, with its long straight avenues and [2]*boiling / marvellous* buildings. The weather in the city can be extreme: the heat in summer can be [3]*deafening / dreadful* and there can be very low temperatures in winter. It snowed while we were there, so Central Park was [4]*deafening / gorgeous* all covered in snow, but I had to buy a new hat and gloves because it was [5]*freezing / boiling*! We took the subway to Wall Street – the noise of the trains was [6]*deafening / enormous*, but it was [7]*stunning / fascinating* to see so many people from all around the world living together in this [8]*enormous / dreadful* city.

2 ☆☆ **Complete the sentences with the adjectives from Exercise 1.**

1 Can I borrow your gloves? My hands are *freezing*.
2 Turn down that music! It's ________.
3 I couldn't watch the end of that horror film. It was ________.
4 Mrs Griffin's a very interesting teacher and her history classes are ________.
5 I didn't realise the London Eye was really this big! It's ________!
6 When we were in Turkey in July it was ________ – 39°C!!
7 Paul had a ________ holiday – he went to Sweden and Norway and he had a great time.
8 Ana's brother is a fashion model – he's totally ________!
9 The view from the top of the mountain was absolutely ________.

3 ☆☆☆ **Complete the sentences so they are true for you.**

1 When it's boiling in summer, I ________.
2 When it's freezing in winter, I ________.
3 The most terrifying experience I've ever had was when I ________.
4 You can get a stunning view of my town / city if you go to ________.
5 A fascinating fact that I know is ________.

A virtual reality tour

5.01 **4** ☆ **Listen to a virtual tour of the Eiffel Tower. Match the numbers (1–5) with what they refer to (a–e). (See the *Learn to learn* tip in the Student's Book, p62.)**

1 1889	c	a pieces
2 1887		b visitors
3 300		c year of the World Fair
4 18,000		d height in metres
5 7 million		e year building was begun

5.01 **5** ☆☆ **Listen again. Answer the questions with two to four words.**

1 What is the first image in the tour?
The original drawing
2 How long after the French Revolution did they build the Eiffel Tower?
____
3 What were the professions of the men who helped Gustave Eiffel?
____
4 Where were the pieces of the tower produced? ________
5 When it was finished, what did the Parisians call the Eiffel Tower?
____

6 ☆☆☆ **Look up some facts about the Eiffel Tower. Write three things you found out about it.**

____
____
____

LANGUAGE IN ACTION

Question tags and questions with prepositions

1 ★ Match the sentences (1–6) with the question tags (a–f).

1 It's freezing, [d]
2 You stayed at a hotel in London, [ ]
3 She won't waste any money, [ ]
4 Mark's got red hair, [ ]
5 You can't solve this maths problem, [ ]
6 This museum doesn't attract a lot of people, [ ]

a will she?
b can you?
c didn't you?
d isn't it?
e does it?
f hasn't he?

2 ★★ Complete the sentences with the correct question tags.

1 We don't have to go to school tomorrow, __do we__?
2 Pat and Tim have got tickets for us too, ________?
3 Clara listens to a lot of music, ________?
4 You'll send me a message when you get there, ________?
5 Laura can speak Spanish, ________?
6 Ahmed has never been to London before, ________?

3 ★ Complete the questions with the prepositions in the box.

about	for	from	~~like~~	of	to

1 Who does your brother look __like__?
2 What is the film *The Avengers* ________?
3 Who did they deliver the pizzas ________?
4 What will this information be used ________?
5 What are spiders webs made ________?
6 Where did all this sand come ________?

4 ★★ Complete the questions with the correct words.

1 Don't worry. What are you scared __of__?
2 He can't be serious, ________ he?
3 The food ________ be collected later, won't it?
4 What's wrong? What are you looking ________?
5 Euan clearly doesn't like Fiona, ________ he?
6 Who were these beautiful pictures created ________?

5 ★★★ Use the prompts to write questions with question tags or with prepositions.

1 A Hi Tomás. call / you / Tom / ?
__I can call you Tom, can't I?__
B Yes, of course. Everyone calls me Tom.

2 A I'm sorry, my English isn't very good.
B where / you / come / ?
____

3 A That's a gorgeous bag. what / made / ?
____
B It's wool. It's a traditional Peruvian bag. I bought it last year.

4 A We're going out for a pizza after class. you / come with us / ?
____
B Yes, of course. See you later.

6 ★★★ Write four sentences with question tags you could use to start a conversation with a person you've just met for the first time.

____
____
____
____

WRITING
A competition entry

1 ★ **Read the competition entry. Which of these topics is not mentioned?**

1 Origins of the city ☐
2 Population ☐
3 Famous places to visit ☐
4 The food ☐

THE BEST CITY I'VE EVER VISITED

HOME | STORIES | PHOTOS

London attracts millions of visitors and on my last visit I understood why. It's a fascinating city and it has many marvellous places to visit.

The first town was built there by the Romans around 2,000 years ago on the River Thames. The city grew and now has a population of almost 9 million people! London is enormous – this is the fact that impressed me most and you are reminded of it when you fly into one of its airports.

There are lots of places to visit in the city, but the highlight of any visit to London is the London Eye. This huge Ferris wheel was opened in 2000 and is located next to the Thames, near Westminster Bridge. It moves around very slowly, but when you finally get to the top you are 135 metres high, and the views from the top are stunning.

I'm absolutely certain that London deserves to win because it has so many incredible places to visit! Without a doubt, London is the best city in the world to visit!

2 ★★ **Read the entry again and answer the questions.**

1 How old is London?
Over 2,000 years old.
2 What impressed the writer about the city?
____
3 Where is the London Eye?
____
4 How tall is it?
____
5 Why does London deserve to win the competition?
____

3 ★★ **How does the writer express these ideas? Find the *Useful language* phrases in the text.**

1 What was most amazing
this is the fact that impressed me the most
2 the best part of a visit
____
3 it should win
____
4 I'm sure
____
5 It is certain
____

Write a competition entry.

PLAN

4 ★★ **Think of the best city you have ever visited. Make notes in your notebook about these things.**

- A short introduction to the city
- General facts about the place
- A detailed description of what impressed you
- Why the place should win

WRITE

5 ★★★ **Write your competition entry. Remember to include four paragraphs, extreme adjectives and expressions from the *Useful language* box (see Student's Book, p65.)**

CHECK

6 **Do you …**

- give an introduction?
- describe its highlights?
- explain why you think the place should win?

5 REVIEW

VOCABULARY

1 Match the words in the box with the definitions (1–8). There are two words you don't need.

boiling create deafening dreadful enormous freezing gorgeous measure solve waste

1 very cold ______
2 make something new ______
3 to use too much of something ______
4 very loud ______
5 find the answer to ______
6 find out the size of something ______
7 very bad ______
8 very beautiful ______

2 Circle the correct options.

1 My phone is *connected* / *communicated* to the wi-fi, but the video's not playing.
2 Alison thought the film was *fascinating* / *boiling*, but I fell asleep after 20 minutes.
3 Some of the scenes in the horror film were *gorgeous* / *terrifying* – I couldn't watch.
4 What time will my new computer be *solved* / *delivered* tomorrow?
5 Olives are *collected* / *supplied* by shaking the tree really hard so that they all fall on the ground.
6 The wedding was *deafening* / *marvellous*, and the bride's dress was *stunning* / *terrifying*.
7 Lots of insects were *developed* / *attracted* by the smell of the food.
8 Several *enormous* / *freezing* rocks fell from the side of the mountain.

LANGUAGE IN ACTION

3 Complete the text with correct passive form of the verbs in brackets.

Help us fix the castle

Originally, to build the old castle, enormous rocks 1 ______ (collect) from the mountains near here and they 2 ______ (deliver) by teams of hundreds of people pulling them. The thick walls 3 ______ all ______ (create) by hand and the rocks 4 ______ (measure) very carefully because they had to go together perfectly.

Now all the rocks are lying on the ground, so each rock 5 ______ (pull) up and then it 6 ______ (drop) in the right place. We're making good progress.

Next year, we will start on the roof. The roof 7 ______ (make) of wood. Trees from the local forest 8 ______ (cut) down and then they 9 ______ (bring) here.

4 Complete the sentences with question tags.

1 It's a gorgeous day, ______?
2 We can't connect the printer, ______?
3 Emily hasn't worked out the answers, ______?
4 Dennis didn't collect the book, ______?
5 These problems will be solved, ______?
6 Rosanna doesn't waste any time, ______?
7 All the pieces of the table have been measured, ______?
8 Bees produce honey, ______?

CUMULATIVE LANGUAGE

5 Complete the conversation with the missing words. Circle the correct options.

EMILIA What [1]__________ to do for the physics presentation next week?

GEORGE I'm not sure. I [2]__________ do something about the tallest buildings.

EMILIA That's … err … different. I mean … doing something about the stars and planets is easier, [3]__________?

GEORGE Well, I [4]__________ this documentary about the Jeddah Tower yesterday – it's in Saudi Arabia. When it's finished, it's going to be the tallest building they'll [5]__________.

EMILIA How tall is the one in Dubai?

GEORGE The Burj Khalifa? That's only 828 metres tall. This one will be [6]__________ bigger! They [7]__________ to make it a mile high – that's 1.6 kilometres, but there were too many problems with that. They think it'll be over one kilometre.

EMILIA Seriously? That's [8]__________ enormous. But what do you mean 'they think'?

GEORGE Well, it could be [9]__________ taller than one kilometre. They're not sure yet.

EMILIA I [10]__________ believe they actually don't know. Someone [11]__________ know.

GEORGE Well, of course but it's a secret, I think.

EMILIA So when are they going to finish it?

GEORGE Well, [12]__________ on it since 2013 and they [13]__________ it for around seven years.

EMILIA That's amazing, isn't it?

GEORGE Yeah … and to think the tallest thing in the world [14]__________ the Eiffel Tower.

EMILIA Anyway, so what does all this have to do with the physics presentation?

	a	b	c	d
1	a do you do	b you will do	c are you going	d may you do
2	a must	b should	c mustn't	d might
3	a it is	b doesn't it	c isn't it	d won't it
4	a had watched	b used to watch	c watched	d have watched
5	a have never built	b ever build	c have ever built	d already have built
6	a rather	b far	c really	d quite
7	a have planned	b had planned	c have been planning	d will have planned
8	a really	b extremely	c a lot	d a little
9	a pretty	b absolutely	c quite	d a bit
10	a mustn't	b don't have to	c shouldn't	d can't
11	a doesn't	b must	c can't	d may
12	a they've been working	b they're working	c they work	d they'll be working
13	a 'll build	b 're going to build	c 'll be building	d build
14	a would be	b is	c used to be	d had been

6 NO LIMITS

VOCABULARY

Verb collocations with *get*, *take* and *have*

1 Complete the table with the words and phrases in the box.

advantage of   a lot out of   an interest in   bored   doubts   fun   ~~lost~~   on my nerves   pleasure in   risks   the chance   to know

get	have	take
lost		

2 Match the beginnings of the sentences (1–6) with the ends (a–f).

1 Oscar has really been getting [a]
2 Harry actually takes [ ]
3 How did you get [ ]
4 Osman really got [ ]
5 I had never taken [ ]
6 Chefs shouldn't take [ ]

a on my nerves lately.
b lost on your way to school?
c risks when they're chopping food – they might cut themselves!
d an interest in doing anything dangerous before.
e pleasure in eating really spicy food.
f a lot out of his time in Liverpool – his English is a lot better.

3 Complete the conversation with one word in each gap.

MIA What's the matter?
ROSE It's Laura again. She's really [1] getting on my nerves.
MIA What's she done?
ROSE Well, I'd just like her to take an interest [2] ______ the things I like doing. She just says she [3] ______ bored when she's with my friends.
MIA That's not fair. She should try getting to [4] ______ them. She [5] ______ the chance to join our group at the party on Friday and she didn't take advantage [6] ______ it. She just stood in the corner on her own!
ROSE Exactly! When we go out with her friends, I always try to [7] ______ fun. I'm having [8] ______ about our friendship!

4 Complete the sentences so they are true for you (see the *Learn to learn* tip in the Student's Book, p71.).

1 When I get lost I ______.
2 It really gets on my nerves when ______.
3 I always have fun when I ______.
4 I once had the chance to ______ but I didn't do it!

Explore it!

Guess the correct answer.
What is the most dangerous job in the world?

a a lumberjack (a person who cuts down trees)	b a firefighter	c an astronaut

Find out an interesting fact about dangerous jobs.

READING

An article

1 ☆ **Read the text. Which two places have Mari and Patricio lived in?**

2 ☆☆ **Look at the words in bold in the text. Use them to complete the sentences.**

1 A long time ago, humans used to ___hunt___ for all their meat.

2 My dad keeps all our bikes in a small ________ in the garden.

3 I find that very hard to believe. It sounds ________ .

4 In the desert, we met a ________ who lived in tents.

5 Eliza ________ that she made a mistake.

6 There are lots of interesting animals and plants in the ________ .

3 ☆☆ **Read the text again and (circle) the correct options.**

1 What is writer trying to do in this text?

a Encourage people to visit Ecuador.

b Give her opinion of Patricio and Mari's relationship.

c Show how difficult it is to live in England.

(d) Explain why Mari decided to go and live in Ecuador.

2 What does the writer think of Mari's actions?

a She agrees that they are ridiculous.

b She admires Mari because she wasn't afraid.

c She finds it hard to believe.

d She's amazed by the story of how Mari met Patricio.

3 Patricio went back to Ecuador because he …

a found a job building houses.

b wanted to spend more time with his daughter.

c didn't like living so far away from his people.

d couldn't find work in Essex.

4 What does Mari think about her new life?

a It's not easy for her because everything is different.

b She misses the life she had in London.

c It's difficult because she can't catch fish.

d She would like to go back to her family and business.

Moving to the jungle

If you had the chance to give up everything to go and live in the Amazon jungle, would you do it? You would certainly have to be very brave, but 52-year-old Mari Muench took the risk.

Her story, which even she describes as 'completely **ridiculous**,' started in 2010 when she was on holiday in Ecuador. There she met Patricio, who is a shaman in his **tribe**. Patricio asked Mari to dance and, as they got to know each other, he told her an amazing story. He said that when he was just 15 years old, he had a dream in which he saw her. Mari also felt a very strong attraction to the place. 'Unless I come to live here with Patricio,' she thought, 'I'll never be happy.'

A few months after this first meeting, Mari and Patricio got married! Then, they decided to move to Essex near London where their daughter Samai was born. But Patricio had many doubts about living so far from his community.

So, Patricio moved back to Ecuador and took advantage of the time there to begin making preparations for Mari and Samai's arrival. With help from his tribe, over a period of four months, he cleared a small piece of land in the **rainforest** and built a traditional **hut**, using only materials from the forest, his hands and a lot of hard work.

In 2018, she left her Essex home, her family and her successful go-karting business, as well as all the advantages of modern life for the Ecuadorian jungle. After a two-day journey, they reached Patricio's community. Mari is learning how to **hunt** and fish, eat insects and share her life with her new family. 'It's the hardest thing I've ever done,' she **admits**, but she says she's very happy.

4 ☆☆☆ **What do you think life will be like for Mari, Patricio and Samai? Write four sentences.**

____

____

____

____

LANGUAGE IN ACTION

First and second conditional

1 ☆ **Match the beginnings of the sentences (1–5) with the ends (a–e).**

1 If you had the chance, [d]
2 We'll almost certainly get lost [ ]
3 Unless he pays attention, [ ]
4 Harry would work harder [ ]
5 If you had a blog, [ ]

a he won't get a lot out of Mr Smith's classes.
b I would read it.
c unless we stop and ask someone.
d would you fly in a helicopter?
e if you encouraged him more.

2 ☆☆ **Complete the second sentence so that it means the same as the first. Use no more than three words.**

1 In case of any doubts, you can call me.
If you ___have___ any doubts, you can call me.

2 Without taking risks, you'd get really bored.
You'd get really bored if you ______ ______ any risks.

3 You don't like Ali because you don't really know him.
You'd really like Ali if you ______ ______ to know him.

4 I'll put the cat out in the garden if it annoys you.
I'll put the cat out in the garden ______ ______ on your nerves.

5 You can get a lot out of playing team sports.
______
team sports, you can get a lot of them.

3 ☆☆ **Complete the conversation with the correct form of the verbs in brackets.**

GRETA What are you doing, James?
JAMES I'm making pizza. If you [1] ___'re___ (be) nice to me, I [2] ______ (give) you a slice.
GRETA Great. But if you [3] ______ (put) pineapple on it, I [4] ______ (not eat) it.
JAMES Well, if you [5] ______ (not like) pineapple, I think I [6] ______ (put) some extra chunks on it!
GRETA Come on, James. If I [7] ______ (make) a pizza, I [8] ______ (not use) any ingredients you didn't like.
JAMES That's true – but you don't cook! If you ever want to learn, I [9] ______ (help) you.
GRETA Oh, please. You only know how to make pizza! If I [10] ______ (take) an interest in cooking, I [11] ______ (ask) Mum or Dad to help me.
JAMES Right, that's it! Extra chunks of pineapple!

4 ☆☆ **Underline and correct one mistake in each sentence.**

1 If I have a drone, I would fly it really fast. ___had___
2 If you folded your clothes properly, your room won't be such a mess. ______
3 Will we get lost if we won't follow the map? ______
4 If I listen to classical music, it might be inspire me. ______
5 Unless you don't try it, you'll never know what it's like. ______
6 What you would do if you had doubts about your future? ______

5 ☆☆☆ **Complete the sentences with your own ideas.**

1 If I knew how to cook well, ______.
2 If I had a blog, ______.
3 I would take more risks if ______.
4 Unless I fail all my exams, ______.
5 If I get a really good job, ______.
6 If I get bored later, ______.

VOCABULARY AND LISTENING

Inspiration and challenge

1 ☆ **Find nine more words for challenges in the word search.**

E	N	C	O	U	R	A	G	E	I	D	G
N	F	A	P	T	X	C	N	I	R	E	D
I	N	S	P	I	R	E	T	A	S	T	C
B	E	R	O	B	S	T	A	C	L	E	H
X	O	(B	R	A	V	E	R	Y)	B	R	A
Q	V	T	T	O	R	Z	T	T	O	M	L
P	E	F	U	U	T	Y	B	G	O	I	L
U	R	C	N	R	G	U	D	V	Y	N	E
A	C	H	I	E	V	E	W	O	R	A	N
L	O	T	T	P	V	I	S	A	E	T	G
V	M	W	I	P	L	D	A	Q	W	I	E
B	E	X	E	R	W	A	U	X	D	O	K
R	U	S	S	U	P	P	O	R	T	N	E

2 ☆☆ **Match the words in Exercise 1 with the definitions.**

1 You'll need this in a dangerous situation. _bravery_

2 My parents do this so that I read more books. ______

3 You'll have to go around or over it. ______

4 Your family and friends will always do this. ______

5 An extraordinary person does this to other people. ______

6 You'll need to work hard when you have one. ______

7 When you keep trying and never give up, you have this. ______

8 You do this if you deal with something successfully. ______

9 If you're lucky, you have these. ______

10 When you reach your aim you do this. ______

3 ☆☆☆ **Write a paragraph about someone who acted with bravery. You can write a true story or invent one.**

______

______

______

______

A radio show

6.01 **4** ☆ **Listen to the radio show about what British people think is 'risky behaviour'. Put the pictures in the order you hear about them.**

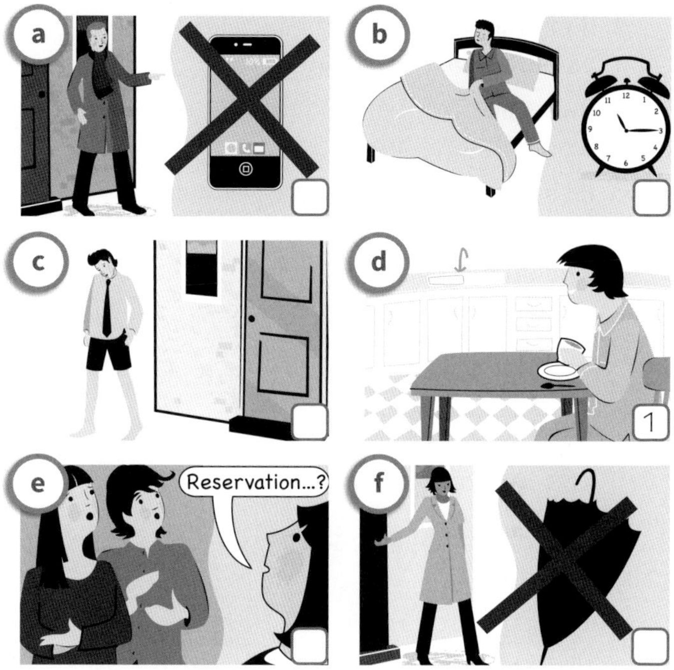

6.01 **5** ☆☆ **Listen again and (circle) the correct options (see *Learn to learn* tip in the Student's book, p74.).**

1 The number of people who took part in the survey was …
  (a) 2,000. b over 2,000. c 40.

2 British people think it's risky to drink coffee or tea before …
  a going out. b having breakfast. c going to bed.

3 What do British people think is risky when they go to a restaurant?
  a Ordering foreign food.
  b Going without booking a table.
  c Booking a table after 11 pm.

4 What shouldn't you do with your mobile phone?
  a Leave it charging for too long.
  b Take it everywhere you go.
  c Leave it at home.

5 British people also think it's risky to leave the house …
  a with different shoes or socks.
  b with wet hair.
  c in their pyjamas.

LANGUAGE IN ACTION

Third conditional

1 ☆ **Match the sentences (1–4) with the pictures (a–d).**

1 If Charlie had missed the bus, he wouldn't have met Hannah. [D]

2 If Charlie hadn't missed the bus, he wouldn't have arrived late. [ ]

3 If I hadn't gone to the party, I wouldn't have had so much fun. [ ]

4 I would have gone to the party if I hadn't agreed to watch a film with Suzy. [ ]

a

b

c

d

2 ☆☆ **Complete the sentences with correct form of the verbs in brackets.**

TO: Aisha

FROM: Amy

Hi Aisha,

I'm never going to have a party in my house again!! First of all, if I [1] hadn't invited (not invite) so many people, there [2] ________ (be) more food for everyone. Then, Carmen and Elsa [3] ________ (not get) lost if I [4] ________ (send) them a map. I don't think inviting Harry was a good idea either. If he [5] ________ (not jump) on the sofa, he [6] ________ (not break) the mirror in the living room.

There was one good thing. If Mira [7] ________ (not come), she [8] ________ (not bring) her friend Beatriz. She's from Turkey, and she invited me to stay with her when I go travelling this summer!

Amy

3 ☆☆☆ **Complete the second sentence so that it means the same as the first. Use no more than three words.**

1 Holly didn't have the same opportunities as everyone else, so she didn't go to university.

If Holly had had the same opportunities as everyone else, she would have gone to university.

2 George didn't take any interest, so he failed the exam.

If George had taken an interest, he ________ failed the exam.

3 The fish didn't taste very nice because of the sauce.

The fish ________ better if it hadn't had that sauce.

4 My friend Mike went to hospital last week because he broke his leg playing football.

Mike wouldn't have gone to hospital if he ________ his leg playing football.

5 The party turned out really well because the music was amazing.

The party wouldn't ________ out so well if the music hadn't been so amazing.

4 ☆☆☆ **Answer the questions with your own ideas.**

1 What would you have done if you hadn't come to school today?

____

2 If you'd been born 50 years ago, what would your childhood have been like?

____

WRITING

A for and against essay

1 ☆ **Read the essay. Is the writer in favour of or against taking risks?**

____

A life without risks is boring

A It's difficult to imagine a life without risk. [1] ___For___ example, we take risks every day when we leave the house. In fact, doctors say your home is the most dangerous place in the world!

B [2] ________ the one hand, some people take pleasure in dangerous situations. For [3] ________, they think that if they don't do something dangerous [4] ________ as climbing mountains, they'll get bored. Some people argue that they are overcoming obstacles with determination.

C On the [5] ________ hand, many people would rather have a quiet life. They don't need to challenge themselves every day. [6] ________, they say that you can get a lot out of life by having fun without taking risks.

D [7] ________ conclusion, it seems to me that if you live your life worrying about the dangers around you, you'll never be happy. However, I personally [8] ________ you shouldn't take too many risks. You only live once, they say. That could mean 'take risks because you've only got one life.' But it can also mean that you should stay alive if you can.

2 ☆☆ **Complete the essay with the *Useful language* phrases.**

believe	~~for~~	furthermore	in	instance	on	other	such

3 ☆☆ **Read the essay again. Complete the sentences.**

1 Doctors say our homes are ______________________.
2 Some people get bored if they don't ______________________.
3 Many people would prefer ______________________.
4 'You only live once' can mean ____________ or ____________.

4 **Read the essay again. Which paragraph (A–D) …**

1 explains the reasons against the argument? ☐
2 summarises the writer's general opinion? ☐
3 introduces the argument ☐
4 explains the reasons for the argument? ☐

Write your own for and against essay.

PLAN

5 ☆☆ **Look at the essay title and make notes on your arguments in favour of and against the statement.**

Life is just about having fun.

In favour:

____

____

____

Against:

____

____

____

6 ☆☆ **Decide what information to include in each paragraph. Use the information in Exercise 4 to help you.**

WRITE

7 ☆☆☆ **Remember to include four paragraphs, conditional tenses, vocabulary from the unit and expressions from the *Useful language* box (see Student's Book, p77).**

CHECK

8 **Do you …**

- include an introduction?
- talk about the arguments for and against?
- have a conclusion?

6 REVIEW

VOCABULARY

1 Complete the expressions with *get*, *have* or *take*.

1 ________ on my nerves
2 ________ advantage of
3 ________ fun
4 ________ risks
5 ________ bored
6 ________ doubts
7 ________ an interest in
8 ________ a lot out of
9 ________ pleasure in
10 ________ to know
11 ________ lost
12 ________ the chance

2 Complete the sentences with the words in the box.

achieve bravery challenge determination encouraged inspired obstacles opportunities overcome support

1 We went to the stadium on Saturday to ____________ our football team.
2 When Paul moved to Moscow, the biggest ____________ was learning to speak Russian.
3 If you fail this test, they won't give you any more ____________ .
4 My parents ____________ me to learn the piano and now I'm a professional musician.
5 Rescuing that dog from the river took a lot of ____________ .
6 We were losing 3–0, but our ____________ helped us to come back and win 3–4.
7 Amy was ____________ to write this song by things that happened when she was young.
8 Everyone has to ____________ many ____________ throughout their lives – that's life.
9 Hassan had to work very hard to ____________ his dream of becoming a dancer.

LANGUAGE IN ACTION

3 Put the words in the correct order to make first and second conditional sentences.

1 I / the teacher / the answer / I'd ask / If / didn't know
____
2 have to / If / you / Peter / have / ask / you'll / any / doubts
____
3 message / send / you / If / I / bored / get / I'll / a
____
4 you / dreams / you'll / Unless / achieve / your / never / try harder
____
5 risky / I / do / it / wouldn't / was / I / thought / it / If
____
6 anything / this obstacle / You'll / you / never / overcome / unless / achieve
____

4 Complete the third conditional sentences with the correct form of the verbs in brackets.

1 If I ________________ (get) lost, I ________________ (not arrive) on time.
2 He ________________ (do) better in the race if you ________________ (encourage) him more.
3 Steve ________________ (not say) anything if you ________________ (not get) on his nerves.
4 I ________________ (not be) able to buy a new phone if I ________________ (not save) all my pocket money for months!
5 If you ________________ (not sit) at the back of the classroom, you ________________ (hear) everything the teacher said.

CUMULATIVE LANGUAGE

5 Complete the interview with the missing words. Circle the correct options.

INTERVIEWER So why did you decide to become a footballer?

GIULIA I suppose it's like everyone. I [1]________ love playing when I was a child. I always had fun playing football. But if I [2]________ the support of my family, I would never [3]________ a professional.

INTERVIEWER [4]________ hard for you up to now?

GIULIA Yes, sometimes. When I was younger, I had doubts about my ability. But then my coach [5]________ an interest in me and I [6]________ to improve and to get [7]________ better than I was. I knew I [8]________ improve my skills if I wanted to achieve my dreams.

INTERVIEWER You don't get bored with football, [9]________ ?

GIULIA No, I don't. [10]________ pleasure in training and my teammates really inspire me. I wouldn't be happy [11]________ I wasn't training and playing football and there are thousands of people there to support me every week. How [12]________ I get bored?

	a	b	c	d
1	would	used to	could	had to
2	hadn't had	hadn't	haven't had	haven't
3	become	became	have become	to become
4	Is it	Was it	Has it been	Had it been
5	take	took	had taken	might take
6	was encouraged	encouraged	am encouraged	encourages
7	rather	quite	totally	far
8	must	will have to	would have needed	would have to
9	do you	don't you	are you	were you
10	I'm always taking	I was always taking	I've always taken	I could always take
11	if	unless	when	after
12	must	could	should	may

7 KEEP CALM!

VOCABULARY

Feelings

1 ☆ Complete the adjectives with the correct vowels. Then, complete the table with the adjectives.

1 r i d i c u l o u s
2 gr _ t _ f _ l
3 h _ rt
4 d _ wn
5 gl _ d
6 p _ _ c _ f _ l
7 _ ns _ c _ r _
8 _ m _ s _ d
9 _ _ g _ r
10 _ nn _ y _ d
11 h _ p _ f _ l
12 thr _ ll _ d
13 s _ t _ sf _ _ d

positive ☺	negative ☹

2 ☆☆ Circle the correct options.

1 Please don't post that photo. I look *peaceful* / *ridiculous*!
2 What have you done? Why is Emily so *annoyed* / *grateful* with you?
3 Paul needs your help. He's feeling *glad* / *insecure* about his class project.
4 If they knew it was raining, they wouldn't be so *amused* / *eager* to go out.
5 My maths teacher isn't *satisfied* / *hopeful* with my work. She thinks I can do better.
6 Chloe's *thrilled* / *down* because she's getting a new mobile phone.

3 ☆☆ Complete the sentences with correct adjectives from Exercise 1.

1 Lucas is ___hurt___ because you didn't invite him to the party. You should say sorry.
2 I'm so ________ you called because I wanted to ask you something.
3 I like studying in the garden because it's so ________ – all you can hear are the birds singing.
4 Liam's feeling ________ because his best friend has just moved to Germany.
5 The teacher wasn't very ________ by my joke, so she gave me extra homework.
6 We're taking a big risk, but we're all ________ that everything will turn out well.

4 ☆☆☆ Write a sentence describing how you would feel if these things happened to you. Explain why. (See the *Learn to learn* tip in the Student's Book, p83.)

How would you feel if …

1 you had to make dinner for your family?
____
2 one of your relatives gave you some money?
____
3 a friend of yours told you she was moving to another city?
____
4 your teacher told you that you had an exam tomorrow?
____
5 you remembered it was a holiday while waiting for the school bus?
____

Explore it!

Guess the correct answers (choose two options).

Dogs can recognise whether a human is angry or happy by …

a their facial expression. b the words they use.
c the tone of their voice.

Find out about other animals that can recognise human emotions.

READING

A magazine interview

1 ★ **Read the interview. Is this sentence true or false?**

Mindfulness doesn't help students with their exams.

2 ★★ **Match the underlined words in the interview with the definitions.**

1 I can't _concentrate_ if you keep talking. You're getting on my nerves.
2 Humans have five ______________: hearing, sight, taste, smell and touch.
3 Lucas improved his ______________ in tennis with practice.
4 Dr Morgan has written many ______________ about stress.
5 The doctor gave Maya a ______________ painkiller after her accident.
6 The doctor told my dad that he has to ______________ his weight.

3 ★★ **Read the interview again and circle the correct options.**

1 Jeremy Parker says that *concentration* / *mindfulness* can stop people having negative feelings.
2 Mindfulness teaches us to pay more attention to *the present* / *difficult situations*.
3 Meditation is used to *control our feelings* / *make us happy*.
4 When we're depressed, *we sometimes make ourselves* / *other people sometimes make us* feel even worse.
5 Cognitive psychology *studies how mindfulness works* / *can teach people to understand their feelings*.
6 Safari Walk is *not difficult to learn* / *especially good for children*.

4 ★★★ **Answer the questions so they are true for you.**

1 What do you do when you feel down or insecure?

____

2 Would you like to learn more about mindfulness? Why / Why not?

____

Mindfulness for students

Sometimes you're worried and insecure about everything and you can't concentrate. These feelings affect your personal life and your school work and can sometimes get worse. The psychologist Jeremy Parker (and many other experts) suggests using mindfulness.

What is mindfulness?

Mindfulness is a very powerful tool or technique that helps people to concentrate more on here and now. It helps you to stay calm in difficult situations, which you often create for yourself. The technique teaches you to practise breathing and uses meditation to calm you down and understand your feelings and thoughts.

How does mindfulness help?

Everyone has times when they feel down or they feel hurt for some reason. Your mind is full of negative feelings, and there's a voice inside you telling you that you're a failure or that you're useless. Through meditation, you learn not to listen to that voice and after a time … the voice stops. So, you stop worrying about things so much and you avoid thinking those negative thoughts.

What is the science behind mindfulness?

There's an area of psychology called 'cognitive therapy' which helps people to understand how they are thinking and to change it. Mindfulness is based on this, and many studies show that it works. One study, for example, showed that meditating before an exam helps you to get better grades. Another study shows that it reduces stress and worry.

Can you give an example of a mindfulness activity?

There's a simple activity called 'Safari Walk'. It works for children, adolescents and adults, and it's very simple: you walk somewhere and while you're walking you notice everything. You listen to the sounds of birds singing, you look at the colours of things – you use all your senses to be in the moment. And you feel peaceful and happy.

LANGUAGE IN ACTION

Gerunds and infinitives

1 ☆ **Circle the correct options.**

1 *Getting* / *To get* lost on the way to school is not normal.

2 It's important *taking* / *to take* advantage of the opportunities you are given.

3 George says he enjoys *cooking* / *to cook* but he doesn't have time.

4 I tasted the sauce *checking* / *to check* if it was too spicy.

5 She decided not *to wear* / *wearing* her new boots to the party.

6 I'm annoyed about *to lose* / *losing* the game.

2 ☆☆ **Complete the conversation with the correct form of the verbs in brackets.**

MAE [1] *Going* (go) to that mindfulness class was a great idea.

ISA Yes, it was. I'm eager [2] ______ (try) it. I'd like [3] ______ (learn) a few more of Dr Fraser's techniques.

MAE Well, first he told us to practise [4] ______ (breathe) … like this.

ISA Don't forget [5] ______ (hold) it for a few seconds.

MAE I feel a bit ridiculous, but after [6] ______ (do) it a few times I'll feel better.

ISA [7] ______ (learn) something new is always a bit strange at the beginning.

MAE I suppose it is. He suggested [8] ______ (try) it at home on our own before the next meeting.

ISA OK, I'm going home [9] ______ (practise). I'll send a message later [10] ______ (tell) you how I get on.

3 ☆☆ **Complete the sentences with the correct form of the verbs in the box.**

bring	hear	look	~~take~~	win	write

1 After an hour of studying, I stopped *to take* a short break.

2 I'll never forget ______ the cup final last year – I was so thrilled.

3 I remember ______ a strange noise and then all the lights went out.

4 John didn't do his homework because he forgot ______ it down yesterday.

5 Rania stopped ______ at her mobile phone to listen to the news.

6 Did you remember ______ a sandwich to school today? We have an extra class.

4 ☆☆ **Match the sentences with the correct meaning.**

1 I stopped to talk to Matt.

2 I stopped talking to Matt.

3 I forgot to call Lisa.

4 I forgot I called Lisa.

a I stopped what I was doing to talk to Matt.

b I don't talk to Matt anymore.

c I don't remember calling Lisa.

d I didn't call Lisa.

5 ☆☆☆ **Answer the questions so they are true for you. Write full sentences.**

1 Do you enjoy swimming in the sea in summer? Why / Why not?

______

2 What did you forget to do last week?

______

3 Which sport would you be interested in learning to play?

______

4 What do you hope to do when you leave school?

______

5 What things have you stopped doing since you were a child?

______

VOCABULARY AND LISTENING

Expressions with *heart* and *mind*

1 ★ **What word goes on the back of these flashcards? Write *heart* or *mind*. (See the *Learn to learn* tip in the Student's Book, p86.)**

1 put his ______ into it	heart
2 learn something by ______	
3 have something on your ______	
4 break someone's ______	
5 it crossed my ______	

2 ★★ **Complete the text with one word in each gap.**

Making decisions is the hardest thing in the world. I just can't [1] ___make___ my mind up whether I want this or that. And then when I've made a choice, I often have doubts – I'm [2] ______ two minds about whether I've made the right choice. Then, it suddenly [3] ______ my mind that the other one might be better, and I think maybe I should [4] ______ my mind. And when it's something that involves other people, I have to [5] ______ in mind what other people think. Maybe you should choose for me!

3 ★★★ **Answer the questions so they are true for you.**

1 What was the last thing you had to learn by heart?

______

2 What do you do when you can't make your mind up about something?

______

3 Who do you talk to when you have something on your mind?

______

A conversation

7.01 **4** ★ **Listen to the conversation between Jack, Amy and Valerie. What does Jack decide to do?**

______

7.01 **5** ★★ **Listen again and answer the questions.**

1 What will Jack have to do soon?

He'll have to do exams.

2 What does Valerie do after school?

______

3 Why does she do it?

______

4 What does Amy do?

______

5 How did she feel at the beginning?

______

6 Why don't Valerie and Amy support Jack's decision?

______

6 ★★★ **Write about something you do after school. What do you do? Why did you decide to do it? What do you like about it?**

______

______

______

LANGUAGE IN ACTION

Subject and object questions

1 ★ **Complete the subject questions with *Who* or *What*.**

1 A ___Who___ decided to buy this ridiculous present for Harry?
  B It was Flavia.

2 A ________ changed your mind about the T-shirt?
  B The price.

3 A ________ produced such a deafening noise?
  B It was thunder.

4 A ________ wants to learn all those names by heart?
  B Nobody.

5 A ________ enjoyed the concert the most?
  B Oscar did.

2 ★★ **Put the words in order to make questions.**

1 you / exams / do / about / feeling / How / avoid / nervous / ?
How do you avoid feeling nervous about exams?

2 the / crossed / when / mind / your / drone / you / What / saw / ?
____

3 decide / to / shopping / did / with / you / go / Who / ?
____

4 get / is / football / to / match / going / at / Who / bored / a / ?
____

5 you / annoyed / with / did / get / What / so / ?
____

3 ★ **Match the answers (a–e) with the questions in Exercise 2.**

a My sister. She hates going to the stadium. ☐
b I thought it was a bird! ☐
c The computer because it stopped working. ☐
d Berat came with me. I bought these jeans. ☐
e Mindfulness helps me to avoid feeling nervous. [1]

4 ★★★ **Complete the interview. Write questions with *Who* or *What* and the words given.**

A discover / your amazing ability?
[1]*Who discovered your amazing ability?*

B My coach, Alison. She saw me playing one day and told me she'd like to be my coach.

A You used to play football, but now you play tennis. make / you / change / your mind / ?
[2] ________________

B I enjoyed them both, but I had to make up my mind and I just loved playing tennis.

A It hasn't been easy for you. support / you in the difficult times / ? [3] ________________

B My family – they're amazing.

A inspire / you / ? [4] ________________

B I really admire Rafael Nadal.

A Now you're number one in your country. it / feel / like / ? [5] ________________

B It's amazing. I'm thrilled.

A You always seem very calm. get / on / nerves / ?
[6] ________________

B Lots of things, actually. I don't like doing interviews!!

5 ★★★ **Answer the questions so they are true for you. Write full sentences.**

1 What do you often get annoyed with?
____

2 Who calls or send you messages every day?
____

3 Among your friends, who plays a musical instrument?
____

4 Who made dinner at home last night?
____

WRITING

An email reply

1 ★ **Read the emails. Which piece of advice does Daniel not give?**

1 find a good teacher ☐
2 buy an expensive guitar ☐
3 borrow a guitar ☐
4 watch videos ☐

TO: Daniel
FROM: Monica

Hi Daniel

Jack told me that you took up the guitar this year. I'm hoping to learn how to play too, but I'm not sure. Is it very difficult? Any advice?

All the best

Monica

TO: Monica
FROM: Daniel

Hi Monica

I'm so glad you wrote to me. Playing the guitar is fun so [1] _I would recommend_ learning it. It's difficult at the beginning, so [2] ________________ find a teacher. My teacher was really patient, and he never got annoyed with me when I did something silly.

Also, [3] ________________ to borrow someone else's guitar for the first few weeks, until you're sure you enjoy it. [4] ________________, don't go out and buy an expensive guitar and then change your mind. Who wants to waste money like that?

You're probably eager to start learning songs, but first try to learn basic things like where to put your fingers. When you find a teacher, [5] ________________ taking classes more often at the beginning? I took three classes a week to get a good start.

Online videos were really helpful, and I'm grateful to my teacher for suggesting that I watch them.

Anyway, good luck!

All the best

Daniel

2 ★★ **Complete the email with the *Useful language*.**

a Whatever you do
b it would definitely help to
c why don't you suggest
d ~~I would recommend~~
e it might be better

Write an email reply.

PLAN

3 ★★ **Look at Laurie's email and think of pieces of advice.**

Hi

I'm really insecure about my exam, and I'm feeling very nervous. Have you got any advice?

Laurie

Make notes on what you think she should and shouldn't do.

Do: ________________________________

____

Don't: ________________________________

____

WRITE

4 ★★★ **Write your email reply. Remember to include the advice you thought of from Exercise 3, *Useful language* for recommending and suggesting (see Student's Book, p89), and reasons for your suggestions.**

CHECK

5 **Do you …**

- say what Laurie should do?
- say what Laurie should not do?
- think the advice is useful?

7 REVIEW

VOCABULARY

1 Find 12 more feelings adjectives in the word search.

R	B	(E	A	G	E	R)	F	O	L	P	S
I	V	S	N	L	C	V	U	H	U	R	T
D	G	A	N	A	Y	A	I	N	H	V	H
I	R	T	O	D	O	W	N	N	O	P	R
C	A	I	Y	F	R	B	S	J	P	K	I
U	T	S	E	D	T	V	E	U	E	Q	L
L	E	F	D	P	E	A	C	E	F	U	L
O	F	I	A	F	Y	E	U	W	U	K	E
U	U	E	S	C	H	F	R	R	L	J	D
S	L	D	A	M	U	S	E	D	F	U	P

2 Complete the expressions.

1 b _ _ _ _ my heart
2 c _ _ _ _ my mind
3 in t _ _ minds
4 c _ _ _ _ to my heart
5 m _ _ _ my mind up
6 l _ _ _ _ by heart
7 p _ _ my heart i _ _ _ it
8 h _ _ _ got something on my mind
9 b _ _ _ in mind
10 c _ _ _ _ _ my mind

LANGUAGE IN ACTION

3 (Circle) the correct options: gerund (G) or infinitive (I).

1 After verbs like *decide*, *refuse*, *hope* G I
2 After prepositions G I
3 To explain purpose G I
4 After verbs like *avoid*, *enjoy*, *suggest* G I
5 As the subject of a sentence G I
6 After adjectives G I

4 Complete the sentences with the correct form of the verbs in the box.

feel go help learn see waste

1 I enjoy __________ things by heart sometimes.
2 Edward is eager __________ with the preparations for the party.
3 Mindfulness can help you to avoid __________ nervous.
4 I don't remember __________ to the hospital after the accident.
5 __________ time is very easy when you have a mobile phone in your hand.
6 I connected these two cables __________ what would happen.

5 Complete the questions for the interview.

INTERVIEWER [1]When / you / start playing basketball / ?
____
MATT When I was about seven years old.
INTERVIEWER [2]Who / teach / you how to play / ?
____
MATT My dad. He loves basketball.
INTERVIEWER [3]Who / give / you your first basketball / ?
____
MATT My coach, actually. Until then I'd always played with my dad's ball.
INTERVIEWER [4]Who / be / your favourite player / ?
____
MATT LeBron James. Of course.
INTERVIEWER [5]What / make / you feel insecure / ?
____
MATT Doing interviews. I never know what to say.
INTERVIEWER [6]Where / you / practise / ?
____
MATT At school. We have a very good gym.

CUMULATIVE LANGUAGE

6 Complete the text with the missing words. Circle the correct options.

Birds come to town

A small town, called Broken Hill in New South Wales, Australia, has a problem. A group of emus – large Australian birds that can't fly – have decided [1] ______________ in the city. It [2] ______________ in the region for many months, and vets believe the birds [3] ______________ be looking for food and water. [4] ______________ along the main street of the town is [5] ______________ strange. You can see the emus stopping to eat in gardens. The vets in the area believe the birds [6] ______________ food and water by local people and now, of course, the emus aren't very eager to leave town. Bruce Wilson, a police officer in Broken Hill, says, 'If it [7] ______________, they wouldn't have come. But if people didn't give them food, they [8] ______________. This isn't a natural place for them.' Local people are afraid some of the birds [9] ______________ by dogs. 'What [10] ______________ if an emu is killed by a car?' asked another neighbour.

	a	b	c	d
1	a living	b live	c lives	d to live
2	a doesn't rain	b hasn't rained	c hasn't been raining	d isn't raining
3	a might	b can	c should	d had to
4	a To walk	b Walk	c Walking	d Walks
5	a too	b a lot	c extremely	d absolutely
6	a have been giving	b have been given	c have given	d are giving
7	a rained	b has rained	c will rain	d had rained
8	a wouldn't stay	b won't stay	c don't stay	d hadn't stayed
9	a are attacked	b will be attacked	c might attack	d attacked
10	a will happen	b had happened	c happened	d does happen

8 ADVERTISING

VOCABULARY

Advertising

1 ★ **Complete the crossword. Use the clues.**

Across

3 The name of a type of product.
6 Tell people about your product (on TV or online).
9 A person who is selling something.
10 You write this to give your opinion about a product.
11 A symbol that represents the product.

Down

1 Change how someone thinks about something.
2 A program that stops adverts on your computer.
4 The object or service a company sells.
5 This type of company makes adverts.
7 A word or short phrase linked to a brand.
8 A person who buys something.

2 ★★ **Complete the sentences with the correct form of the verbs in the box.**

advertise	block	~~buy~~	market
not influence	produce	review	sell

1 I don't want *to buy* a new phone. This one's perfectly good.
2 A lot of the people who ______ the book online said they didn't like it.
3 I saw those drones ______ on TV – they look amazing.
4 Some products are very difficult ______ in other countries because of their names.
5 Do you know anyone who ______ a bike? I need a new one.
6 Most technological devices like phones and tablets ______ in Asian countries.
7 A lot of people say that advertising ______ them – but actually it does.
8 There are so many adverts on the Internet that sometimes I'd really like ______ them all.

3 ★★ **Look at the verbs in Exercise 2 again. What is their noun form? (See the *Learn to learn* tip in the Student's Book, p95.)**

1 *buyer* 5 ______
2 ______ 6 ______
3 ______ 7 ______
4 ______ 8 ______

Explore it!

Guess the correct answer.

It's not true that we don't like watching adverts. An advert for Samsung in India has got over ______ million views.

a 100 b 150 c 200

Find an interesting fact about an advert and send a question in an email to a classmate or ask them in the next class.

READING

A report

1 ☆ **Read the report. In what ways can companies find out about our habits?**

____

2 ☆☆ **Match the underlined words in the report with the definitions.**

1 open a webpage access
2 looking through ______
3 collect ______
4 give someone the most recent information ______
5 information, especially facts and numbers ______
6 give or supply something for free ______

3 ☆☆ **Are the sentences *T* (true) or *F* (false)? Correct the false sentences.**

1 We only provide marketing companies with information when we want to.
F We also provide them with information without realising it.
2 GPS is used with social media to record where we are.
______
3 A lot of data is gathered to give users recommendations.
______
4 Public transport systems also gather data about their users.
______
5 We don't generate much more data than we did over 20 years ago.
______
6 Most of the figures in the last section show our internet activity in one minute.
______

4 ☆☆☆ **Answer the questions in your own words.**

1 Do you think companies always use our data to provide us with better services and products?
______
2 Do you think companies know too much about us?
______

HOW DO COMPANIES COLLECT DATA?

As Internet and social media users, we give out lots of personal information about ourselves, which we often want to provide. But there's a lot of information which we don't even realise we're giving away and which marketing companies gather in different ways. When we click on an advert, companies know. They also know about things that we type into a search engine, or the people who we follow and whose photos we are looking at on social media. Through GPS, they also know where we are all the time. Every time you access your social media, your location is registered.

How do companies use our data?

Every time you watch a video on YouTube, that information is used to recommend another video that you might like. The same thing happens with the songs that we listen to on Spotify or the products that we buy online. Brands use data to match buyers to products through advertising. But it's not just about selling things: in cities, data can update us on when the next bus or train is coming or where there's a traffic jam. Nowadays, a lot of people use technology to provide information about their health, which they can use to make important decisions about diet or visits to the doctor.

How much data do we generate?

Three billion people use the Internet and we produce 50,000 GB of data every second! In 1992, that figure was 100 GB of data every day. We spend almost $900,000 on Amazon and download 375,000 apps.

50,000 GB

In one minute people …

- watch 4.3 million videos on YouTube.
- send 187 million emails.
- send 38 million messages on WhatsApp.
- post 481,000 Tweets.

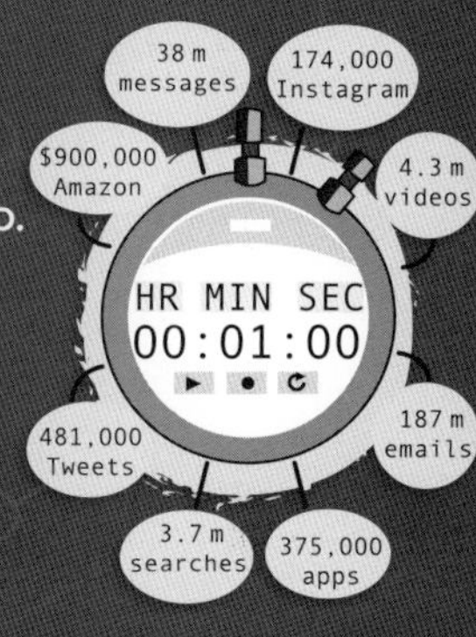

In one minute there are …

- 3.7 million searches on Google.
- 174,000 people browsing photos and videos on Instagram.

LANGUAGE IN ACTION

Defining and non-defining relative clauses

1 ★ **Circle the correct options.**

1 The band *that* / *what* I listen to the most are called the 1975.
2 The logo *that* / *who* the company designed looked like a bird.
3 Tom and George became friends in Santiago *where* / *when* they are both learning Spanish.
4 They work for a company *whose* / *who* products are sold all around the world.
5 Lots of people buy products *when* / *which* they've seen the advert.

2 ★★ **Complete sentences 1–5 with the correct non-defining relative clauses (a–e).**

1 Sophie, _c_, is going to university next year.
2 These products, ___, are sold on beaches in the summer.
3 Freddie used to live at 30 Wilson Road, ___.
4 Our local football team, ___, have just won the league.
5 The advertising campaign, ___, will display the new logo.

a whose shirts are sponsored by my dad's company
b where a famous TV star lives now
c ~~who lives next door to us~~
d which come all the way from China
e which will run from September to December

3 ★★ **Complete the text with the correct relative pronouns.**

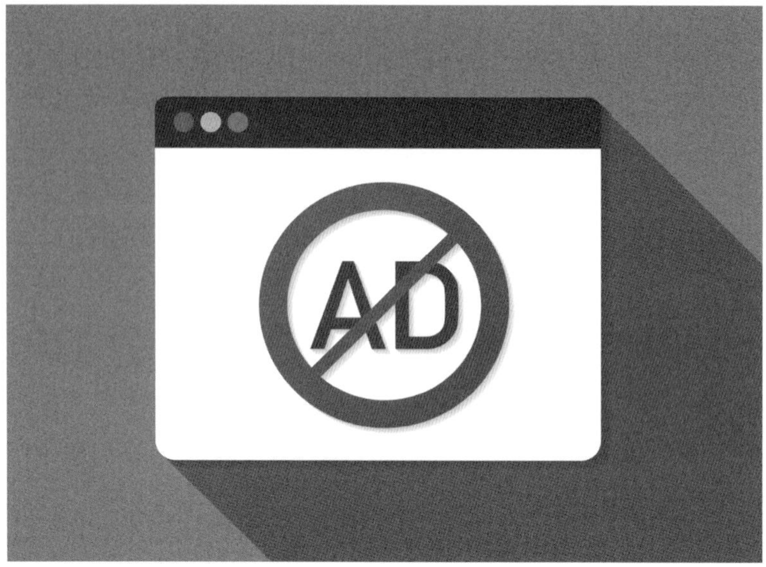

Ad-blockers are software programs [1] _that_ stop adverts appearing on your screen. Many people [2] ________ use the Internet get annoyed with adverts [3] ________ pop up on the screen, but I don't mind them. I quite like seeing adverts from companies [4] ________ products I like. The Internet is a place [5] ________ marketing companies try to market their brands, [6] ________ you might or might not like. I don't remember a time [7] ________ there were no adverts on the Internet. Do you?

4 ★★ **Rewrite the sentences using a relative pronoun.**

1 This is a product. This product sells in around 50 different countries.
This is a product that sells in around 50 different countries.
2 This advert is very funny. I've seen it about five times.
____
3 Mr Cooper is very satisfied with our work. This means we'll pass the course.
____
4 The girl in my class speaks French very well. Her sister lives in Paris.
____
5 London has lots of interesting places to visit. I'm going there for Christmas.
____
6 There's a boy in my chemistry class. He really gets on my nerves.
____

VOCABULARY AND LISTENING An interview

Internet verbs

1 ★ Circle the correct options.

1 Over six million people have subscribed *on* / *to* the Lego channel on YouTube.
2 If I like someone's post, I always comment *on* / *to* it and say something nice.
3 Jenna Marbles vlogs *about* / *of* make-up, her dogs and her daily life. She's got over 18 million followers.
4 Influencers say you have to work very hard to build *on* / *up* a large number of followers.
5 I tried Instagram for a while, but I take terrible photos, so I shut *up* / *down* my account.
6 The app sends you messages about new games, but you can switch *on* / *off* this option if you don't want to see them.

2 ★★ Complete the email with the correct form of the verbs in the box.

build up	comment on	delete	follow	post
shut down	~~subscribe~~	switch on	vlog about	

Dear subscriber,

Thank you for [1] _subscribing_ to our YouTube channel. You can also [2] ______________ us on Twitter and Instagram. Over two years we have [3] ______________ over one million followers thanks to you.

On this channel we will be [4] ______________ our favourite video games. If you would like to [5] ______________ the videos, we'd love to hear from you, and we'd love you to [6] ______________ ideas for new vlogs. If you follow us on Twitter, you can [7] ______________ the option to receive new messages from us on your screen. Remember, rude posts will be [8] ______________. If you continue to make rude comments, your account will be reported and it might be [9] ______________.

3 ★ Guess which numbers in the box match the sentences.

50 million	5 billion	over 1 billion
over 65 million	~~2005~~	

1 The year YouTube started. _2005_
2 The number of YouTube users. ______________
3 The number of people making videos. ______________
4 The number of videos watched every day. ______________
5 The number of subscribers to PewDiePie's YouTube channel. ______________

4 ★★ (8.01) Listen to an interview about the YouTube video channel. Check your answers to Exercise 3.

5 ★★ (8.01) Listen again. Are the sentences *T* (true) or *F* (false)? Correct the false sentences

1 Three young men started YouTube after an argument at a dinner party.
F They decided they wanted to share videos from a dinner party but found it difficult.
2 Janelle believes that young people watch YouTube more than TV.
____
3 Product review videos are not that popular.
____
4 People watch YouTube to find out how to do things or how good thing are.
____
5 PewDiePie makes documentaries.
____

LANGUAGE IN ACTION

Indefinite, reflexive and reciprocal pronouns

1 ☆ **Circle the correct options.**

1 Someone / *Anyone* posted this video about my village.
2 I don't know *nobody* / *anybody* who vlogs about video games.
3 I swear I didn't delete *anything* / *something* from your computer.
4 What's that noise? Is *anybody* / *nobody* there?
5 He's just joined Instagram, but *anyone* / *no one* follows him yet.
6 I switched the computer on, but *anything* / *nothing* happened.

2 ☆☆ **Complete the text with the words in the box.**

anything ~~nobody~~ nothing (x2) someone (x2) something (x2)

Be careful with what you post on social media because [1] *nobody* likes rude comments. My gran used to say, 'If you have [2]______ nice to say, don't say [3]______.' If you disagree with [4]______, tell them and explain why. There's nothing wrong with disagreeing about [5]______, but you can really hurt [6]______ if you're unkind. If you can't discuss [7]______ politely, then say [8]______.

3 ☆ **Circle the correct options.**

1 She might have hurt *himself* / *herself* when she fell.
2 You shouldn't get annoyed with *yourself* / *ourselves* for something like this.
3 How do I look? I'm going to take a photo of *myself* / *yourself*.
4 Paul and I met *ourselves* / *each other* at a party two years ago.
5 We really enjoyed *ourselves* / *themselves* on our holidays.
6 It was a difficult project, so they decided to help *themselves* / *one another*.

4 ☆☆ **Cross out and correct one mistake in each sentence.**

1 This sport is totally safe. ~~Anything~~ dangerous can happen to you. *Nothing*
2 Anna taught himself how to vlog about video games. ______
3 Phil and I are really good friends. We talk to ourselves about everything. ______
4 There isn't nothing you can do about adverts on TV except switch them off. ______
5 It's nothing serious – I just cut me with a knife. ______
6 I don't know no one at this party. Is there anyone you know here? ______

5 ☆☆ **Complete the text with the correct indefinite or reflexive pronouns or *each other*.**

My sister went to live in Canada last month to work at a big marketing company. We send messages to [1] *each other* almost every day and she tells me [2]______ about her life there. She says she's enjoying [3]______, but at first it was difficult because she didn't know [4]______ in Toronto and she had to do everything [5]______ without any help. She found a flat in the city centre, but there was [6]______ in it – not even a bed! She lives with another girl now, but they hardly ever see [7]______ because the other girl works at night. But at least she has [8]______ to talk to sometimes. We all miss her!

WRITING

An online product review

1 ☆ **Read the review of an app. What does the writer particularly like about it?**

____

2 ☆ **Complete the *Useful language* phrases in the review with the words in the box.**

allows ~~designed~~ features included missing

App Reviews

Search

Home News Reviews Top apps Sign in Register

Review: PhotoStar app

A PhotoStar is a new app for mobile phones. If you love taking photos with your phone but you think they're a bit boring, you should try this app.

B PhotoStar is [1] *designed* to be used on photos on your mobile phone or tablet. It [2] ________ you to add funny features to your photos like emoticons, animations and elements like glasses, beards or funny ears. One of its best [3] ________ is that you can add voice messages using the voice of someone famous. So, you can send a funny photo to your friend that has a message with your favourite celebrity's voice. I tried out all the different features and sent some photos to my friends. All of them wanted to know the name of the app. The one thing that's [4] ________ is a better text function so that you can also write funny messages or slogans on your photos. One is [5] ________ with the app, but it isn't very interesting.

C PhotoStar is free and it has no annoying adverts. It offers more features in the paid version, which is very cheap. I've recommended it to all my friends.

STAR RATING ★★★★

3 ☆☆ **Read the review again. In which paragraph (A–C) can you find the following?**

1 A negative point. [B]
2 A summary of the app. [ ]
3 A description of the app. [ ]
4 Specific features of the app. [ ]
5 A recommendation. [ ]

Write a review of an app.

PLAN

4 ☆☆ **Choose an app to review. Think of the positive features. What do you think is missing? Decide what information to include in each paragraph. Use Exercise 3 to help you.**

WRITE

5 ☆☆☆ **Write your review. Remember to include a title and three paragraphs, language from this unit and expressions from the *Useful language* box (see Student's Book, p101).**

CHECK

6 **Do you …**
- give a star rating?
- say what you like and don't like about it?
- say whether or not you would buy it?

8 REVIEW

VOCABULARY

1 Complete the sentences with the words in the box.

ad-blocker advert advertise brand buyer influenced logo marketing product review seller slogan

1 If you are not satisfied with the __________, please return it in 15 days.
2 I can't remember the __________ name, but I know it was yellow.
3 Our company's __________ is 'We work harder for you.'
4 You can see the company __________ on the back of the phone.
5 Everyone loved the __________ that was shown on TV last Christmas.
6 The products that they __________ on this website are all video games.
7 He works for a __________ company with offices all around the world.
8 A lot of children are __________ by adverts on TV.
9 We found a __________ for our old car.
10 A __________ will often want to charge a higher price for the product.
11 I use an __________ so I don't see any adverts on websites.
12 Bea always writes a __________ of the products she buys online.

2 Match the beginnings of the sentences (1–8) with the ends (a–h).

1 On Twitter, I like following ☐
2 Dave has just posted ☐
3 If you don't want people to comment on your video, ☐
4 As an influencer, Lydia has built up ☐
5 I don't know why I subscribe ☐
6 Lately, Lucas has been vlogging ☐
7 If you don't delete ☐
8 They wouldn't have shut down ☐

a you can switch that option off.
b your account if you hadn't posted those terrible things.
c about that new video game – it looks amazing.
d some photos of the party – he looks so funny.
e accounts that post information about football.
f that photo, I'm never going to speak to you again!
g to this channel – I don't even like rap music.
h a lot of followers since last year.

LANGUAGE IN ACTION

3 Complete the text with the correct relative pronoun.

The simplest technique [1] __________ marketing companies use to sell their products is repeating its name again and again. This technique, [2] __________ is most common on the radio, often doesn't explain the product. On TV, perfume companies, [3] __________ products are all very similar, use a slightly different technique, [4] __________ is to have a stunning image of a beautiful man or woman [5] __________ says the name of the brand at the end. On the Internet, [6] __________ there is often no sound, this technique is hardly ever used.

4 **Complete the sentences with a reflexive pronoun, or *each other.***

1 Did you hurt ________ when you dropped all those books?

2 I heard Larry talking to ________ while he was in the bathroom.

3 Diana didn't ask for help from anyone. She did everything ________.

4 Do you and Peter see ________ every day in class?

5 When you're insecure, you have doubts about ________ and your ability.

5 **Complete the text with the indefinite pronouns in the box.**

anyone	anything	everything	nothing	someone (x2)

My friend said to me the other day that they had seen [1] ________ in an advert that looked like me. I've never been in an advert and I don't know [2] ________ who has. I watched the advert myself and the person looked [3] ________ like me at all. [4] ________ about her was different – her hair, her face … there wasn't [5] ________ about her that I could see that was similar to me. Maybe they were thinking of [6] ________ else.

CUMULATIVE LANGUAGE

6 **Complete the text with the missing words. Circle the correct options.**

A man called Thomas J Barratt [1] ________ the father of modern advertising. In 1865, Barratt started working in the Pears soap company [2] ________ he created a system of advertising with works of art by [3] ________ famous British painters to advertise the soap. One of the most famous paintings [4] ________ was of a young boy, clearly from a rich family, with a bar of Pears soap in his hand – the soap [5] ________ to the original painting. Barratt knew that [6] ________ Pears soap in people's minds with quality would create a better image. He believed that the product [7] ________ have a good slogan. The company used the slogan, 'Good morning. Have you used Pears soap?' for well over 60 years. He also thought that if the company put Pears soap adverts everywhere – on buses, in magazines and on posters – [8] ________ would see the adverts. However, Barratt also knew that things went out of fashion quickly and advertising [9] ________ change too. Modern advertising has kept many of Barratt's ideas and it [10] ________ his techniques ever since.

1 a considers b considered c has considered d is considered

2 a which b where c when d that

3 a totally b a lot c quite d a little

4 a used b was using c have used d had used

5 a added b had been added c had added d was adding

6 a connect b connected c connecting d connects

7 a has to b ought to c must have d can

8 a anybody b no one c someone d everyone

9 a had to b must c could d have to

10 a is using b was using c has been using d use

9 HAVE YOU HEARD THE NEWS?

VOCABULARY

Reporting verbs

1 ☆ **Find 11 more reporting verbs in the word search.**

R	E	F	D	E	N	Y	U	R	S	E
C	L	A	I	M	O	F	A	E	U	A
O	I	N	S	I	S	T	D	F	G	N
N	O	U	C	S	I	E	M	U	G	N
F	A	P	O	L	O	G	I	S	E	O
I	C	W	V	G	G	E	T	E	S	U
R	F	K	E	E	R	Z	I	U	T	N
M	V	P	R	O	M	I	S	E	D	C
C	O	M	P	L	A	I	N	F	O	E

2 ☆☆ **Match reporting verbs from Exercise 1 with the direct speech sentences.**

1 'No, the government is not going to close any more hospitals.' ___deny___
2 'Yes, it's true what you've heard. Our star player is leaving the team.' ________
3 'I've told you a hundred times. I don't know who Kevin is.' ________
4 'Why don't you look it up on Wikipedia?' ________
5 'No, I'm not doing it. I'm not going shopping with you.' ________
6 'I hate watching ads before videos. They're so annoying.' ________

3 ☆☆ **Complete the story with the reporting verbs in the box. (See the *Learn to learn* tip in the Student's Book, p107.)**

admit announced ~~apologise~~ claimed discovered promised

Giles had to [1] ___apologise___ to all his followers for telling a big lie! On his vlog, Giles [2] ________ that he had been asked to play in a video game competition. He [3] ________ that the designers of the video game wanted him to play. At the end of his vlog, he [4] ________ to tell everyone all about it the following week. So, we waited for his vlog. Nothing happened. He didn't appear. When the competition came, we all watched, but he wasn't there either. That's when we [5] ________ that he was lying. Giles had to [6] ________ it had all been a lie. He has lost a lot of followers … including me.

4 ☆☆☆ **Write a sentence using the reporting verb and your own ideas about a time when …**

1 a teacher announced something.

____

2 someone refused to do something.

____

3 a friend apologised.

____

4 someone promised that they would do something for you.

____

5 you complained about something.

____

Explore it!

Guess the correct answer.

The first 24-hour news channel was CNN, which started in

a 1980 b 1995 c 2000

Find an interesting fact about a news channel or website. Send a question in an email to a classmate or ask them in the next class.

READING

A newspaper story

1 ★ **Read the newspaper story. Choose the best summary.**

a Police solve the mystery of 'Piano Man' ☐
b 'Piano Man' tells his story ☐
c 'Piano Man': too many questions remain ☐

2 ★★ **Match the <u>underlined</u> words in the newspaper story with the definitions.**

1 a problem, events or a person that is dealt with by the police *case*
2 strange or not understood ______
3 a person who plays the piano ______
4 walking slowly in no particular direction ______
5 of no use, or value ______
6 very well, in a very pleasant way ______

3 ★★ **Read the story again. Answer the questions.**

1 What was strange about the man when he was found?
He didn't say anything.
2 Why did the hospital think he played the piano?
______
3 Why did police think he came from Norway?
______
4 Why weren't they able to solve the case?
______
5 How did the man get home?
______
6 What is a 'Hollywood ending'?
______

4 ★★★ **What do you think about this story? What was the man doing?**

______
______
______
______

The strange <u>case</u> of 'Piano Man'

In 2005, a very strange story hit the news. Newspapers and TV stations reported that a young man had been found <u>wandering</u> the streets in a town in Kent, England. He was wearing a suit and tie, but he refused to speak.

He was taken to a hospital and the doctors insisted that he was in good health but that he didn't speak. Then he drew a picture of a piano, so people suggested that he might be a <u>pianist</u>. A piano was taken to the hospital and some newspapers claimed that he played the piano <u>beautifully</u> and that he seemed to be happy.

The nurses asked him where he was from, but he still didn't say anything until one day he pointed to Oslo on a map. The police announced that it was possible that he might come from Norway. They discovered that a ship had travelled from Norway to England when the man was found. Did he jump from the ship and swim to the English coast? The police asked a Norwegian speaker to talk to him, but she told them that he hadn't spoken to her either. One newspaper claimed that he wasn't able to talk at all.

TV and radio stations and newspapers asked everyone to help them to find out who the <u>mysterious</u> 'Piano Man' was. Police admitted they had received a lot of calls, but all the information that people gave was <u>useless</u>.

Unfortunately, there's no Hollywood ending to this story. The man was actually Andreas Grassl, a 20-year-old from Germany, who returned there with his parents. Police discovered that he could actually talk. But what was he doing? Why was he in Kent? How did he get there? Why didn't he say anything? Why were all these stories told about him? It all remains a mystery.

LANGUAGE IN ACTION

Reported statements and commands

1 ☆ **Are the sentences reported commands (*C*) or statements (*S*)?**

1 My sister told me not to worry. C
2 Hector refused to tell me where he was. ___
3 I told Carla that I would meet her later. ___
4 Sandra insists that she didn't know about the party. ___
5 She told us to wait for her after class. ___
6 My parents told me to stay at home tonight. ___

2 ☆☆ **Rewrite the sentences using the correct form of the reporting verbs in the box.**

~~admit~~ announce complain deny refuse tell

1 'All right, it was me. I dropped my drink and it fell on your bag.'
Helen admitted that she had dropped the drink.
2 'I hate washing-up. Why do I always have to do it?!'
My brother ______
3 'Look, it wasn't me. I would never send you a message like that.'
David ______
4 'I'm not going to talk to Ryan ever again!'
Mia ______
5 'Listen, everyone. Tomorrow there's going to be an exam.'
The teacher ______
6 'Go home and lie down. You'll be fine in a few hours.'
The doctor ______

Reported offers and suggestions

3 ☆ **Are the sentences offers (*O*) or suggestions (*S*)?**

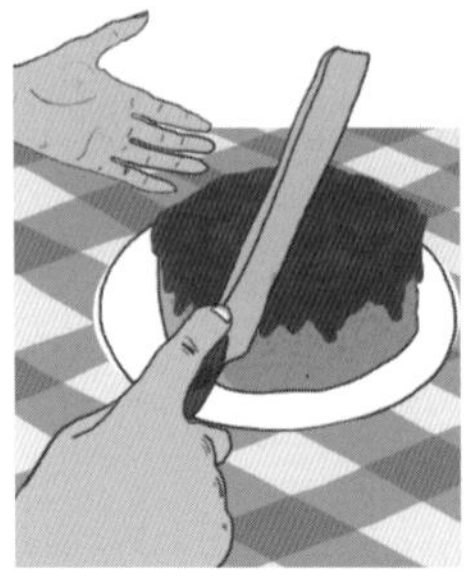

1 I'll slice the cake in half if you like. O
2 Why don't you check online if there are any good films on? ___
3 I can lend you a nice shirt if you need one. ___
4 I'll hold your bag while you try on the sweater. ___
5 Shall we meet after class and discuss your progress? ___
6 Why don't I ask my dad if he'll give us a lift. ___

4 ☆☆ **Rewrite the sentences in Exercise 3. Use the reporting verbs *offered* or *suggested*.**

1 Alison offered to slice the cake in half.
2 Tim ______
3 Ayaz ______
4 She ______
5 The teacher ______
6 Ada ______

5 ☆☆☆ **Write sentences that are true for you about …**

1 something you tell your parents not to do.
______
2 something you promised a friend you would do.
______
3 a time when you denied doing something.
______
4 a suggestion you made to your friend.
______
5 something that you always refuse to do.
______

VOCABULARY AND LISTENING

Adverbs of time and manner

1 ★ Complete the sentences with the adverbs in the box.

after a while | eventually | fluently | gradually | occasionally | ~~patiently~~ | regularly | secretly | surprisingly

1 I waited *patiently* at the cinema for an hour, but Tim never turned up.

2 Emily only __________ posts photos on social media because she doesn't take many photos.

3 They claimed that they had __________ downloaded people's personal data without anyone knowing.

4 No one has ever heard of him in my country, but __________ he has over one million followers in Japan.

5 At first, I couldn't see anything, but __________ my eyes __________ got used to the dark and __________ I saw the house in the distance.

6 Our French teacher speaks six languages __________, and he __________ travels to Japan because he's also learning Japanese!

2 ★★ Complete the story with the adverbs from Exercise 1. Sometimes more than one answer is possible.

Paul stood beside the tree and waited [1] *patiently* for the animal rescue people to arrive. He looked up [2] __________ to check that the bird hadn't moved. It was a beautiful creature. A large eagle, Paul thought, but he wasn't sure. [3] __________ the bird tried to take off, moving its wings, but not [4] __________ it couldn't get anywhere because one of its wings was broken. Paul [5] __________ wished he could speak bird language [6] __________, so he could tell it that everything would be fine. [7] __________, a white van arrived. A man and woman got out. They approached the bird slowly and [8] __________ so as not to scare it. The woman threw a large blanket over it and they [9] __________ managed to get it into a large cage. They thanked Paul and offered to take him home, but he said no and walked home looking at the photos on his phone.

A radio interview

9.01 **3 ★ Listen to an interview about viral videos. Which of these reasons does the man not give for sharing a video?**

They're useful. ☐

It causes positive or negative feelings. ☐

It makes us laugh. ☐

It's important to us. ☐

It has a story. ☐

9.01 **4 ★★ Listen again. Complete the notes with key words and information.**

1 Jonah Cook is a *marketing manager*.

2 There are __________ things you need to do to communicate well.

3 We like to watch a good story until __________ to find out what happens.

4 'How-to' videos are __________ because they help us to do something.

5 There are lots of videos with __________ which show you how to build up followers.

6 We share 'how-to' videos because it makes us look __________.

5 ★★★ Send a message to a friend and compare your answers. (See the *Learn to learn* tip in the Student's Book, p110.)

LANGUAGE IN ACTION

Reported questions

1 ★ Complete the reported questions with one word in each gap.

1 My teacher asked me where I ___was___ going.
2 She asked me ________ I was chatting to.
3 The coach asked me what my favourite sport ________.
4 Nicolas asked me ________ I wanted something to eat, but I told him I wasn't hungry.
5 Molly wanted to know if I ________ gone to the party last Friday.
6 Euan asked me if he ________ come to my house to watch the match later.

2 ★★★ Rewrite the reported questions in Exercise 1 in direct speech.

1 '___Where are you going___?' my teacher asked me.
2 '________________?' she asked.
3 '________________?' the coach wanted to know.
4 '________________?' Nicolas asked, but I told him I wasn't hungry.
5 '________________?' Molly wanted to know.
6 '________________?' Euan asked me.

3 ★★ Put the words in order to make reported questions.

1 was / where / asked / the station / We / a police officer
We asked a police officer where the station was.
2 asked / My / been / I'd / where / dad / me
____
3 help / Paul / I / his / bike / me / if / asked / could / fix / him
____
4 tomorrow / to school / ask / me / if / She / didn't / I / was / going
____
5 asked / Marco / me / I'd / Brooke / seen / when
____

4 ★★★ Below are five questions an interviewer asked a famous rock star. Complete Oliver's email to his friend about the interview.

a Why did you start playing the guitar?
b What was your favourite subject at school?
c Are you happy with your latest album?
d Will you play a song for us?
e When is your next tour?

Hi

There was an interview with Jimmy B last night on the TV. It was cool! First, they asked him [1] ___b___. He said it was maths!! Then they asked him [2] ________. He said his dad had a guitar and he just picked it up one day. Later on, they asked him [3] ________, and he said he thought it was his best album so far. I can't wait to hear it. They also wanted to know [4] ________ and guess what? He's coming to Birmingham next May! We HAVE to go! And then they asked him [5] ________, and so he picked up his guitar and he played my favourite *Straight to Blue*. It was amazing! See you tomorrow!

Oliver

5 ★★★ Think about questions your parents or teachers have asked you this week. Write them using reported speech.

My mum asked me if I had tidied my bedroom!
____
____

WRITING

A news story

1 ☆ **Read the news story. How do the children communicate in the village of Ubang?**

____

2 ☆ **Match the sentences (1–5) with the paragraphs (A–C). Two sentences match one of the paragraphs.**

1 An expert's explanation of the Ubang languages. [B]
2 An explanation given by the Ubang chief. [ ]
3 A fear about the future. [ ]
4 A general belief about communication between men and women. [ ]
5 Examples of different words that Ubang men and women have for things. [ ]

3 ☆☆ **Complete the news story with the *Useful language* phrases in the box.**

asked insisted that Nowadays said ~~surprisingly~~

What did you say?

A People, especially older people, often complain that men and women don't understand each other. But there is a Nigerian village where men and women actually do speak different languages because, [1] surprisingly , they use different vocabularies for many things. Ubang people are proud of their language and culture but are afraid that the language will not continue.

B In the village of Ubang, women use the words *okwakwe* for 'dog' and *ogbala* for 'cup' and men say *abu* and *nko*. And there are many other examples of words that sound different and use completely different letters. When [2] ____________ if men and women find it difficult to understand each other, the Ubang village chief [3] ____________ everyone understands each other perfectly and that they are very proud of the difference. In fact, there are lots of words that men and women have in common. Ms Chi Chi Undie, who has studied the community, says that the men and women of the tribe live very separate lives. 'All their children are brought up speaking the women's language fluently,' she [4] ____________ . When the boys get older, they learn to speak like the men in order to be closer to them.

C [5] ____________, most children are learning English and the older members of the community ask what is going to happen to their unique language situation. … The village chief is determined that it will survive because, he says, 'if the languages die, the Ubang people will exist no more.'

Write a news story.

PLAN

4 **Research a current news story on a few websites to get difference versions. Make notes on these things in your notebook.**

A general introduction
The basic facts of the story (who? what? where?)
An interesting fact or extra information
Quotes from the people involved

WRITE

5 **Write your news story. Remember to include three paragraphs, language from this unit and expressions from the *Useful language* box (see Student's Book, p113).**

CHECK

6 **Do you …**

- include an interesting headline?
- include some extra details in the third paragraph?
- include some direct speech?

9 REVIEW

VOCABULARY

1 Complete the sentences. The first letter is given.

1 Sarah s________________ that we buy a present for James.
2 I said he was lying and he a________________ I was right.
3 Julia c________________ she met Lionel Messi, but I don't believe her.
4 Remember that you p________________ you would help me move my bed later.
5 The students are c________________ that the classroom is too cold.
6 Francesca d________________ that she had fallen asleep in class, but everyone could see her.
7 The president a________________ that he was going to visit our school.
8 Ricardo still hasn't a________________ for breaking my watch.
9 The teacher d________________ that Sophie used a mobile phone in the exam.
10 Thomas has always i________________ that nobody told him about the trip to France.
11 I can't believe that you are r________________ to talk to Victoria because she lost your jumper.
12 The school principal c________________ that the art teacher had had an accident.

2 Circle the correct options.

1 Isaac *patiently* / *secretly* hid the box, and nobody knows where it is.
2 I only *gradually* / *occasionally* clean my computer. I should do it more often.
3 They waited *patiently* / *eventually* in the queue for hours, but there were no tickets left.
4 My dad has a friend who speaks eight languages *nowadays* / *fluently*!
5 I saved two euros every week and *regularly* / *gradually* I saved enough money for a new phone.
6 *After a while* / *Nowadays* hardly anyone uses public telephones in the street.
7 The doctor says that my dad should take exercise more *regularly* / *occasionally*.
8 The film was interesting at the beginning, but *secretly* / *after a while* I got bored and fell asleep.
9 I thought the meal would be very expensive, but it was *surprisingly* / *patiently* cheap.
10 Mark sent a message to say he was late and *eventually* / *gradually* he arrived at 11.30.

LANGUAGE IN ACTION

3 Match the beginnings of the sentences (1–6) with the ends (a–f).

1 We asked the teacher if ☐
2 The police told everyone ☐
3 Lucas asked me what ☐
4 My parents suggested ☐
5 Beatrice offered ☐
6 The magician explained ☐

a I was doing later.
b that I had to remember the card I had in my hand.
c to clear the area because there was a big fire.
d to help me fix my bike.
e we had to write in pen or pencil.
f going to the beach for the weekend.

4 Complete the second sentence so that it reports the first. Use no more than three words.

1 'Can you look it up on the Internet?' Ivan asked me.
Ivan asked me ____________ look it up on the Internet.

2 'What did Josh say in the message?' Sara asked her.
Sara asked her what ____________ in the message.

3 'Will you invite me next time?' Ann asked me.
Ann asked me ____________ invite her next time.

4 'Where are you waiting for me?' asked Bella.
Bella asked me ____________ waiting for her.

5 'How did you know the answer?' Leo asked us.
Leo asked us ____________ the answer.

6 'Do you need directions to the station?' asked the police officer.
The police officer asked us ____________ directions to the station.

CUMULATIVE LANGUAGE

5 Complete the text with the missing words. Circle the correct options.

SCIENCE NEWS: Goats prefer happy faces

Everyone loves a happy animal, [1] ____________? Scientists in England [2] ____________ that goats are attracted more by happy faces than by angry ones. It suggests that goats, like other animals [3] ____________ humans keep at home or on farms, [4] ____________ read human faces and understand human feelings. Previous studies had [5] ____________ shown similar results in tests [6] ____________ were done with horses and dogs.

In the tests, the reactions of the goats were studied by [7] ____________ them in a closed area. Then different faces [8] ____________ to people who gave them pasta to eat, [9] ____________ is their favourite snack. The goats went to the happy faces more often and spent [10] ____________ more time studying the faces with their noses. They also found that if they changed the faces from men to women, it [11] ____________ any difference to the goats. Scientists believe the results [12] ____________ us to understand animals better in the future.

	a	b	c	d
1	doesn't it	does he	don't I	don't they
2	just have discovered	have discovered just	have just discovered	have just discover
3	what	that	if	to
4	can	should	ought to	can't
5	still	never	yet	already
6	who	that	where	whose
7	put	to put	putting	puts
8	attached	are attached	were attaching	were attached
9	which	what	that	who
10	quite	a lot	fairly	totally
11	makes	would make	didn't make	hadn't made
12	were helped	help	helped	will help

EXAM TIPS: Listening skills

Listening Part 1: Multiple-choice pictures

You will listen to short extracts and choose from different options. This exam task tests your ability to listen for specific information and answer questions about what you hear.

Exam guide: Multiple choice

- If the question is about a dialogue between a boy and a girl, underline which of the two people you need to answer the question about. For example: *What food will the boy eat?*
- Decide if the question is asking about the past, present or future. The verb tense and time expressions in the question will help you. For example: *What is the weather like now?* is a completely different question from: *What will the weather be like tomorrow?*
- Listen carefully to see if the meaning is positive or negative. For example: *Can you buy some fruit – but not bananas?* tells us that the speaker does not want bananas.
- Usually the answer will come in the middle or at the end of the listening and not at the beginning. This means that you should always wait until the end of each listening before you choose your answer.

REMEMBER!

Don't choose a picture as an answer just because you hear information about it in the listening. Usually you will hear information related to all three pictures!

Listening practice: Multiple-choice pictures

Tip!

Listen for key words or synonyms to help you identify the answer.

1 Choose the correct meaning for the expressions.

1 Are you kidding me?
   A I don't believe you. B That's interesting!
2 You're getting on my nerves.
   A You're funny! B You're irritating me!
3 You'll never know unless you try.
   A You should try. B Are you going to try?
4 You're coming to my party, aren't you?
   A Are you sure you're coming to my party?
   B Can you confirm that you're coming to my party?
5 You must feel really proud of your exam results!
   A I'm sure you feel really happy about your exam results.
   B You ought to feel very happy about your exam results.
6 I get a lot out of playing chess.
   A Playing chess is hard for me. B I really enjoy playing chess.

2 You will hear six short extracts. Are the sentences *T* (true) or *F* (false)?

E.01

1 The boy's sister irritates the girl. ___
2 The speaker says everyone should study abroad. ___
3 The boy's coffee is very hot. ___
4 There is a present in the box. ___
5 Some fruit tastes better than it smells. ___
6 The girl thinks going to university is a bad idea. ___

Tip!

Sometimes information later in the listening will contradict or correct the information before. For example:
A: *Amy loves skateboarding.*
B: *Well, that was before her accident. She hasn't done it since then.*
This is another reason why you need to wait till the end before choosing your answer.

3 **Listen to the conversation between Ben and his mum. Answer *Yes* or *No*.**

E.02

1 Are the dishes washed? ___
2 Does Ben need to do his homework tonight? ___
3 Is Ben going to speak to his friends tonight? ___

4 **Listen again. What is Ben going to do first? Choose the correct option A, B or C.**

E.02

EXAM TIPS: Reading skills

Reading Part 2: Multiple matching

Matching people with activities and things

You will read descriptions of people and match them with the best options. Remember that there may be more options than people, so read carefully! The extra options usually fit only partially, not completely.

Exam guide: Multiple matching

- Begin by reading the five descriptions of the people. Underline the key information in each description.
- Next, read all eight texts carefully and underline the key information in each one.
- Then compare the underlined information in the description of the first person with the underlined information in the texts. Which text is the best match for this person?
- Don't choose a text just because it repeats some words from the description of one person. You need to focus on the meaning of the descriptions and the texts and not on individual words.

REMEMBER!

Be very careful when choosing – the text needs to be a perfect match for everything the person wants.

Reading practice: Multiple matching

Identifying meaning

1 Choose the option (A, B or C) that shows the meaning of the first sentence.

1 Jack wants to do without chocolate for a week.

A Jacks wants to eat less chocolate for a week.

B Jack thinks he can do without chocolate for a week.

C Jack would like not to eat chocolate for seven days.

2 Chloe is looking forward to learning to drive.

A Chloe plans to learn to drive.

B Chloe is happy that she will start driving soon.

C In the future Chloe will learn to drive.

3 Liam has moved to Liverpool.

A Liam is living in Liverpool now.

B Liam has travelled to Liverpool.

C Liam is spending some time in Liverpool.

Synonyms

2 Match the underlined words with the synonyms in the box. There are four extra words.

be born	can	cook in oil	cook in the oven	cut into pieces
heat	know	lived as a child	think	will possibly

1 I'm going to bake a cake. ____________
2 Jon grew up in Chicago. ____________
3 How long does it take to fry the onions? ____________
4 Rachel might go to university. ____________
5 I guess they must be brother and sister. ____________
6 You need to chop the peppers. ____________

Tip! Don't look for words that match exactly. Read the text carefully and underline synonyms of the key information words.

Eliminating options

3 Read what Laura wants. Then decide which option(s) (A–D) you can eliminate.

Laura wants to buy a new mobile phone. It must be the latest model, transparent, feel very light and smooth and have a very large display.

A We repair all the latest models of mobile phones …
B Our shop has a good selection of mobile phones, including classic old models …
C We have the latest models. They're transparent, very light and have big displays. We're definitely the best place to get a new watch.
D This shop specialises in all sorts of digital devices. Its products are expensive, but they look great!

Tip! When you think you have a correct answer, check the incorrect options again to be sure that they don't match.

Finding differences

4 Read about Sam and Nathan. Find three differences between them.

Sam wants to try out some new recipes. He cooks every day. During the week he hasn't got much time to cook, but he's got time at the weekend to make more complicated dishes. He doesn't eat fried food or food with a very strong flavour.

Nathan likes very spicy food. He wants to buy a book of recipes. He is especially interested in making quick meals in the frying pan.

____

____

____

EXAM TIPS: Listening skills

Listening Part 3: Gap-fill

In this part of the exam, you have to listen and complete notes or sentences. The notes or sentences summarise what you hear. You have to write a word, number or a very short noun phrase.

Exam guide: Gap-fill

- Pay attention to the instructions. They remind you what you have to do, but more importantly, they tell you what the topic is.
- After the instructions there is a pause. Use this to read the notes or sentences.
- While you read, try to think about what type of word is missing. It might be a day, a number, a date or price, for example.
- The sentences or notes summarise what the speaker says so you are not going to hear what is written on the page. Pay attention to the key words.
- As you listen, write down the words – remember the answers are one word or a very short phrase.
- During the second listening, check your answers.

REMEMBER!

Check that your answers make sense in the context if you are given a second opportunity to listen.

Tip!

The sentences and notes will give you clues about what type of information is missing. Read everything carefully.

LISTENING PRACTICE: Gap-fill

1 **Read the notes. What type of information is missing?**

Hire a bus
Number of seats on our bus: [1] ________
Bus leaves: 10.30 am
Meet at youth club: [2] ________
Price of exhibition entrance: £5
Special group price (over 20 people): [3] £________

2 E.03 **You will hear some information about a visit to a photography exhibition. Listen and write the correct answer in the gaps (1–3) in Exercise 1. Then, listen again and write down the other numbers that you hear.**

____

Tip!

What you read in the exam questions is not what the person says – it is a summary or paraphrase. Think about the meaning and listen for key words.

3 E.04 **Listen and complete the sentences.**

A Angela's mum told her that her ___________ had won the competition many years ago.

B To find out more about the competition, visit the website – www.___________.org.

C Angela entered the competition with her ___________ .

D The class was given a grant of £ ___________ to build their robot.

4 You will hear an announcement about events coming up at a youth club. Before you listen, read the notes in Exercise 5. What type of information is missing from the gaps?

a type of clothing	day	name of food	number	subject	time

5 E.05 **Listen and complete the notes with one or two words or a number or a date or a time.**

Youth club events: November

Weekly cooking classes:

Every [1] ___________ at 5 pm

Mary

1) bake a chocolate cake; 2) roast [2] ___________

Visit 1:

Date: Friday 16th at [3] ___________ pm

Helen Fields – fashion designer

Workshop: match colours; choose jeans; decorate a plain white [4] ___________ (must bring)

Visit 2:

Date: Saturday, 24th at 7 pm

Dr Michael Redding – Professor of [5] ___________

Talk: history of logos

Logo competition:

1st prize [6] £___________ in cash

The passive

Present simple		
Spanish	is	spoken in many countries.
Tigers	aren't	found in Africa.

Past simple		
Writing	was	invented in Asia.
Planes	weren't	used until the 1900s.

will		
The prize	will be	awarded next week.
The food	won't be	served until 10 pm.

Questions			
Will	your project	be	finished by next week?

- We use the **passive** when we don't know or are not interested in who or what does an action.
- To form the **passive**, we use the appropriate form of ***be*** + **past participle**.
  Millions of emails are written every day.
  Brian wasn't invited to the party.
  The microwave will be repaired tomorrow.
- We use the **present simple passive** to talk about facts in the present.
  English is spoken in most hotels and tourist offices.
- We use the **past simple passive** to talk about facts in the past.
  The first video game console was made in 1972.
- We use ***will*** with the **passive** to talk about facts and actions we believe will happen in the future.
  Results will be emailed to students next week.
- We use ***by*** with the **passive** to show who or what was responsible for an action.
  The book was written by a marketing expert.
- To form questions in the present and past, we use the appropriate form of ***be*** + **subject** + **past participle**. We put *Wh-* question words before ***be***.
  Was the light bulb really invented by Edison?
  Where is the most coffee drunk in the world?
- To form questions with ***will***, we use ***will*** + **subject** + ***be*** + **past participle**.
  When will the next drama club meeting be held?

Question tags

Main clause	***be/do/have/*modal + subject pronoun**
They aren't ready,	are they?
They are ready,	aren't they?
We don't need a pencil,	do we?
We need a pen,	don't we?
He was ill,	wasn't he?
He wasn't ill,	was he?
She can't run a marathon,	can she?
She can run a marathon,	can't she?
You won't be late,	will you?
You'll be late,	won't you?
You haven't seen it,	have you?
You've seen it,	haven't you?

- We use **question tags** at the end of statements to invite a response from the listener.
  A: You're an athlete, aren't you?
  B: Yes, I am.
- To create **question tags** we use the main verb ***to be***, auxiliary verbs ***to do*** or ***to have*** or a **modal verb**, plus a **subject**. The subject is normally a pronoun.
- Positive sentences have negative question tags and negative sentences have positive tags.
- When we use the auxiliary *be*, *do* or *have*, a modal verb or main verb *be* in the main clause, this verb is used in the tag.

Questions with prepositions

- When a **question word** is the object of a **preposition**, the preposition usually comes at the end of the clause, especially in an informal style.
  What are you looking for?
  Who is this pizza for?
  Who is he listening to?
  Which programme are you talking about?
  What are you laughing at?
  What's it full of?
- We often form questions with prepositions at the end in passive questions.
  Who was it written by?

The passive

1 Complete the sentences with the passive form of the verbs in brackets.

1 Our shopping _will be delivered_ (deliver) to our house tomorrow morning.

2 These problems ________ (solve) a long time ago.

3 ________ phone batteries ________ (produce) in this factory?

4 A lot time ________ (waste) if we don't do something now.

5 It was delicious. The meat ________ (chop) into small pieces.

6 My computer ________ (not connect) to the wi-fi.

2 Use the prompts to write questions in the passive. Use the tense in brackets.

1 When / the books / deliver / ? (past)

When were the books delivered?

2 Why / flies / attract / to the smell of food / ? (present)

____

3 How / these images / create / ? (past)

____

4 Where / we / collect / after the museum visit / ? (future)

____

5 How / the meat / cook / ? (past)

____

6 When / a time machine / develop / ? (future)

____

3 Rewrite the sentences in the passive.

1 This lake supplies water to our town.

Water is supplied to our town from this lake.

2 They will communicate your grades to you in a week.

Your grades ________

3 We measured the ingredients very carefully.

The ingredients ________

4 They grill the fish over a fire.

The fish ________

4 Complete the text with the passive form of the verbs in brackets.

The city of Dubai is incredible. Before oil [1] _was discovered_ (discover) in 1966, it was a small town, but it [2] ________ (develop) into a modern city where millions of tourists [3] ________ (attract) to its shopping malls. In 1999, the seven-star Burj Al Arab [4] ________ (complete), and the 828-metre tall Burj Khalifa [5] ________ (open) in 2010. A new city with air conditioning [6] ________ (plan) for the future. Hotels and apartments [7] ________ (connect) with seven kilometres of shops.

Question tags

5 Complete the questions with the correct auxiliary verbs.

1 James _isn't_ coming to lunch tomorrow, is he?

2 They ________ have to take the train, do they?

3 You ________ deliver the message later, won't you?

4 Robbie ________ going to call us today, wasn't he?

6 Complete the questions with the correct questions tags.

1 You don't know the answer, _do you_ ?

2 Dad collected his car from the garage, ________ ?

3 Everyone knows the answer, ________ ?

4 They can't see the screen, ________ ?

5 Elena doesn't want to help us, ________ ?

6 You won't tell anyone what I told you, ________ ?

Questions with prepositions

7 Write questions asking about the underlined words. Use the preposition in bold.

1 Grace is listening **to** <u>some classical music</u>.

What is Grace listening to?

2 The class was **about** <u>the main rivers in Europe</u>.

____

3 Logan baked a cake **for** <u>his grandmother</u>.

____

4 The food was delivered **by** <u>a man on a bike</u>.

____

5 My dad's very angry **with** <u>my brother</u>.

____

LANGUAGE REFERENCE

UNIT 6

First conditional

- We use **first conditional** sentences to talk about possible situations in the present or future and say what we think the result will be.
- We often use ***if*** + **present simple** to describe the possible action or event.
  We'll find tickets if we go online at 7 am.
- We can use ***unless*** + **present simple** instead of ***if not***.
  Unless we hurry up, we'll miss the bus.
- We use ***will/won't*** + **infinitive** when we are sure of the result and ***may*** or ***might*** + **infinitive** when we are less sure.
  If we don't leave now, we won't catch the 8.30 train.
  If my uncle doesn't feel better, he may not travel.
- When we use ***if*** to start the sentence, we use a comma between the two parts.
  If I've got enough money, I'll go to the concert.
- We normally use ***will*** to make first conditional questions. It is unusual to use ***may*** or ***might***.
  Will you practise with me this evening if you have time?

Second conditional

- We use **second conditional** sentences to talk about imaginary situations and the possible consequences.
- We use ***if*** + **past simple** to describe the imaginary situation and ***would***, ***could*** or ***might*** for the consequence.
  If I didn't have a cat, I'd like to have a rabbit.
- We use ***would*** **(*not*)** when we are sure of the consequence.
  He would do better in school if he didn't spend all his time playing basketball.
- We use ***could*** **(*not*)** to express a possibility or ability as a consequence.
  If it was Friday night, we could go to the cinema.
- We use ***might*** **(*not*)** to show we are less sure about the consequence.
  If I had more free time, I might take up the guitar.
- We can use ***was*** or ***were*** in the ***if***- part of the sentence with *I*, *he/she* and *it*.
  If it wasn't/weren't so spicy, I could finish it.
  I wouldn't say anything if I were/was you.

Third conditional

Imaginary past situation	**Imaginary past consequence**
(*if* + past perfect)	(*would have* + infinitive)
If I had seen your message,	I would have called you.
If I hadn't seen your message,	I wouldn't have called you.
Imaginary past consequence	**Imaginary past situation**
(*would have* + infinitive)	(*if* + past perfect)
I would have called you	if I had seen your message.
I wouldn't have called you	if I hadn't seen your message.
Questions	
If he had been the chef,	what would he have prepared?
If you had let me help you,	wouldn't you have done better?

- We use the **third conditional** to talk about imaginary situations in the past and the imaginary past consequences.
  If you hadn't read the story, the ending of the film would have been a surprise.
  They would have found the exam easy if they'd worked harder.
- We use ***if*** + **past perfect** to describe an imaginary past situation.
  If I hadn't missed the shot, we would have won the game.
  The book would have been better if the hero hadn't guessed that Jason was the bad guy.
- We use ***would*** **(*not*)** + ***have*** + **past participle** when we are sure of the imaginary past consequence.
  We would have seen his new car if he'd been at home.
  If she'd won the match, she wouldn't have been sad.
- We often use the **third conditional** to talk about things we regret doing.
  If I hadn't posted that photo, my parents wouldn't have found out.
  My sunglasses wouldn't have broken if I hadn't left them on the sofa.

First conditional

1 Match the beginnings of the sentences with the ends.

1 If I get lost on the way,
2 If you season the chicken first,
3 Sean won't come to lunch
4 We might solve the problem quicker
5 Unless you listen to the teacher,
6 They might go sailing

a you won't understand.
b unless we go for a pizza.
c it might taste better.
d unless it rains.
e I'll call you.
f if we sit down and talk.

2 Complete the sentences with the correct form of the verbs in brackets.

1 If you _listen_ (listen) very carefully, you _'ll hear_ (hear) a bird singing.
2 You ________ (not understand) Molly unless you ________ (get) to know her better.
3 Ruby ________ (not have) fun unless she ________ (join) in the game.
4 If Oscar ________ (waste) any more time, he ________ (be) late for school.
5 We ________ (not be) able to watch the video unless we ________ (connect) to the wi-fi.

Second conditional

3 Circle the correct options.

1 If you *had* / *have* a new dog, what *you would* / *would you* call it?
2 If Brian *would go* / *went* to bed earlier, he *wasn't* / *wouldn't* always be late for school.
3 If I *could* / *can* have any job, I *'d work* / *worked* in a chocolate factory.
4 What *would you* / *did you* do if you *would find* / *found* a new mobile phone on the street?
5 If my mum *doesn't* / *didn't* work so hard, I think she *'d* / *'ll* be a lot happier.

4 Use the prompts to write questions.

1 If there / be / no electricity for a week, what / you / do / ?
If there was no electricity for a week, what would you do?
2 If animals / communicate / with humans, what / they / say / ?
____
3 you / go / to Mars / if / you / have / the chance / ?
____
4 What / you / do / all day if you / live / on a desert island / ?
____

Third conditional

5 Complete the sentences with the correct form of the verbs in brackets.

1 If you _had taken_ (take) more interest in the subject, you _wouldn't have failed_ (not fail) the exam.
2 I ________________ (not get) lost if you ________________ (not tell) me to turn left.
3 Henry ________________ (finish) the marathon if we ________________ (encourage) him a bit more.
4 We ________________ (not miss) our stop if we ________________ (not fall) asleep on the bus.
5 What ________________ (happen) if Hannah ________________ (press) that button?

6 Complete the third conditional sentences in the conversation with the correct form of the verbs in the box.

buy	give	go	~~invite~~	look	not have	not hurt

ROSE If Alice [1] _had invited_ you to her party, [2] ________ you ________?
ELA Of course. And I [3] ________ her a nice present for her birthday.
ROSE Really? What [4] ________ you ________ for her?
ELA I probably [5] ________ for something, like some earrings.
ROSE So why didn't she invite you?
ELA It's a long story. But if I [6] ________ her feelings when she needed me to be her friend, we [7] ________ that big argument a few weeks ago.

Gerunds and infinitives

Gerunds

- We can use a **gerund** as a noun and to make noun phrases.
  Running is great exercise.
  My favourite free-time activity is kitesurfing.
  Being the youngest child can be difficult sometimes.
  They think having a school dance is a terrible idea.
- We also use the **gerund** after prepositions.
  My aunt isn't very good at cooking, but she tries very hard.
  They spend a lot of money on buying clothes.
  We're thinking of giving up singing lessons.
  I'm looking forward to seeing you this summer.
- We use the gerund after certain verbs and expressions. Some common verbs and expressions which need a gerund include *avoid*, *finish*, *enjoy*, *practise*, *miss*, *be good/bad at*, *can't stand*, and *don't mind*.
  They enjoy working on the same team.
  I don't mind helping you clean your room.
- With most verbs, we add ***-ing*** to the **infinitive** (without *to*).
  eat – eating *watch – watching* *buy – buying*
- For verbs ending in **-*e***, we remove the **-e** and add ***-ing***.
  have – having *write – writing* *save – saving*
- For verbs ending in a **vowel** and a **consonant**, we double the consonant and add ***-ing***.
  get – getting *run – running* *shop – shopping*

Infinitives

- We usually use the **infinitive with *to*** after adjectives.
  He was lucky to get tickets for the show.
  I'm very pleased to meet you!
  My teacher's very easy to talk to.
- We also use the **infinitive with *to*** after certain verbs. Some common verbs which are followed by an **infinitive with *to*** include *decide*, *want*, *refuse*, *hope*, *would like*, etc,
  Kaitlyn decided to help me with my homework.
  We would like to buy two tickets, please.
  They refused to come with us.
- Some verbs need an object before the **infinitive with *to***.
  My mum taught me to ride a bike.
  I didn't invite Elizabeth to come with us.
- Some verbs can have an object before **the infinitive with *to***.
  They asked us to turn the music down.
  She'd like everyone to arrive by 8 am.
- We can use a **gerund** or **infinitive** after *remember*, *forget* and *stop*, but it changes the meaning.
  Remember to do your assignment. (= Don't forget to do it.)
  Do you remember feeling so happy after we won? (= Do you have a memory of that moment?)

  Don't forget your book bag. (= Bring your book bag.)
  We'll never forget winning that championship. (= We'll always have a memory of that moment.)

  We stopped to eat something on our trip. (= We paused for a moment.)
  They stopped eating junk food last year. (= They quit eating junk food.)

Subject and object questions

- When we use **subject questions**, we are trying to find out information about the subject of the question. We don't use an auxiliary verb (*do*, *does*, *did*), the word order is inverted and the *Wh*-word becomes the subject of the sentence.
  Who ate the last piece of cake?
  What happened?
- When we use **object questions**, we are trying to find out information about the object of the question and we use an auxiliary verb (*do*, *does*, *did*).
  Who does Tania like? (= We want to know who Tania likes.)
  What did Brad want? (= We want to know what Brad wanted.)
- To compare **subject and object questions** that are similar:
  Topic: *Mike likes eating vegetables.*
  Who likes eating vegetables? (subject question) (Who = Mike)
  What does Mike like eating? (object question) (What = likes eating vegetables)

LANGUAGE PRACTICE

Gerunds and infinitives

1 Complete the sentences with the gerund or infinitive form of the verbs in brackets.

1 It's easy _to get_ (get) lost in this city.
2 Kyle refuses ________ (help) me with the project.
3 ________ (be) a police officer can be a dangerous job.
4 My mum has decided ________ (sell) her car.
5 My grandmother enjoys ________ (listen) to the radio.
6 Are you afraid of ________ (fly)?

2 Complete the sentences with the gerund or infinitive form of the verbs in the box.

drive	go	play	~~show~~	solve	take	use

1 I'll be happy _to show_ you around my school.
2 We're looking forward to ________ skiing this winter.
3 Have you finished ________ my computer?
4 Would you like ________ video games later?
5 ________ public transport in big cities is often quicker than ________.
6 This problem might be complicated ________.

3 Complete the email with the correct form of the verbs in brackets.

Hi Hollie

I hope you're well. Do you remember [1] _inviting_ (invite) me [2] ________ (come) and stay with you a few months ago? Well, I'm really pleased [3] ________ (tell) you that I'm going to be in Ireland next month. My parents have decided [4] ________ (send) me to Dublin for a month because they would like me [5] ________ (practise) my English. I don't mind [6] ________ (travel) to Dublin at all. In fact I'm really looking forward to [7] ________ (see) you again.

I really hope [8] ________ (hear) from you soon

Love, Amber

4 Circle the correct options.

1 I don't remember *to tell* / *telling* you what Sarah told me.
2 Have you forgotten *to do* / *doing* your homework again?
3 Samuel can't stop *to listen* / *listening* to that song. He loves it.
4 We worked on the project all day and we only stopped *to eat* / *eating* lunch.
5 I've never forgotten *to win* / *winning* that art competition.
6 Sophie didn't remember *to set* / *setting* her alarm clock so she was late.

Subject and object questions

5 Write subject questions for these answers.

1 William decided not to go to the party.
Who decided not to go to the party?
2 Class 5A is going to the National Museum tomorrow.
____
3 Nobody sent me a message on my birthday.
____
4 A rock fell on my dad's car.
____

6 Circle the correct options.

1 Who *invented* / *did invent* the telephone?
2 What *studies your sister* / *does your sister study*?
3 Who *is going* / *he going* to tell George?
4 What *did happen* / *happened* when she found out?
5 Who *can ask* / *can we ask* to come and help us tomorrow?
6 Which team *beat* / *did you beat* last year?

LANGUAGE REFERENCE UNIT 8

Defining relative clauses

- We use **defining relative clauses** to give essential information about a person, place or thing.
  My aunt has a friend who makes great cookies.
  This is the film that I told you about.
- We use **relative pronouns** at the beginning of relative clauses. We do not repeat the subject pronoun when the subject of the pronoun and following clause are the same.
  They know a lot of people who live in Istanbul.
  They know a lot of people who ~~they~~ live in Istanbul.
- We use ***who*** or ***that*** to talk about people.
  The woman who/that lives next door is very friendly.
  I like the new person who/that works in the café.
- We use ***that*** or ***which*** to talk about things.
  I don't enjoy books which/that have sad endings.
  He wants to buy some boots which/that he can wear with his new hat.
- We use ***where*** to talk about places.
  That's the office where my uncle works.
  Let's go to the restaurant where I had my birthday dinner.
- We use ***whose*** to talk about possessions.
  Do you remember the boy whose mobile was lost?

Non-defining relative clauses

- We use **non-defining relative clauses** to give extra information about a person or thing. We don't need it to understand who or what is being referred to. It is not necessary information. Non-defining relative clauses are introduced by a relative pronoun and we use commas around them.
  Ms Parker, who studied in Italy, is my teacher.
  They just visited Madrid, where Javier is from.
  Last night we had dinner at John's Pizza Parlour, which we'd never tried before.
  My dad, whose name is Wayne, is 40 years old.
- We don't use ***that*** to introduce a non-defining relative clause.
  Sam, who scored three goals in the first game, was amazing.
  ~~Sam, that scored three goals in the first game, was amazing.~~

Indefinite pronouns

anybody	anyone	anything	anywhere
everybody	everyone	everything	everywhere
nobody	no one	nothing	nowhere
somebody	someone	something	somewhere

- We use **indefinite pronouns** to refer to people, places or things in a general way. To create **indefinite pronouns**, we combine *any*, *every*, *no* and *some* with *body*, *one*, *thing* or *where*. We write them as one single word, except for *no one*.
  Is anybody here? = Is anyone here?
  Everybody is late today. = Everyone is late today.
  Nobody was there last night. = No one was there last night.
  Can somebody help me? = Can someone help me?
  Is something wrong? = Is anything wrong?

Reflexive pronouns

I	→	myself	it	→	itself
you	→	yourself	we	→	ourselves
he	→	himself	you	→	yourselves
she	→	herself	they	→	themselves

- We use **reflexive pronouns** when the subject and the object of a verb are the same.
  I sing to myself when I'm alone.
  ~~I sing to me when I'm alone.~~
  She bought herself a new shirt.
  ~~She bought her a new shirt.~~
- We can also use **reflexive pronouns** to emphasise that someone did something alone, without help.
  He didn't buy the cookies – he made them himself. He's good at baking.

Reciprocal pronouns

- We use ***each other*** when each of the two (or more) subjects do the verb to the other subject(s).
  Dave and Ellen sent each other presents. (Dave sent Ellen a present, and Ellen sent Dave a present.)
  The triplets really love each other. They're always together.

LANGUAGE PRACTICE UNIT 8

Defining relative clauses

1 Match the beginnings of the sentences with the ends.

1 Is that the film that — b
2 Rugby is a sport that
3 This is the park that
4 We have a neighbour who
5 This company has a slogan that
6 That's the student whose

a has a big lake in the middle of it.
b stars Daniel Radcliffe?
c says, 'Power to shoes'.
d plays the drums.
e chair broke in French class.
f is played between teams of 15 players.

2 Complete the sentences with the correct relative pronoun.

1 I really like that new advert *that/which* has a song by Mark Ronson.
2 That's the cinema ___________ Mark dropped a whole bucket of popcorn.
3 She's the teacher ___________ laptop was stolen from the classroom.
4 It's a radio station ___________ plays mostly rock and pop.
5 This is the hotel ___________ we stayed on our last holiday.

Non-defining relative clauses

3 Correct the mistake in each sentence.

1 That advert, ~~what~~ was on TV last night, was really funny. *which*
2 This fish, which we bought it in the supermarket, was very expensive. ___________
3 Maya, who's dad comes from Australia, works in marketing. ___________
4 Theo's review of the film, that Lucas sent me, was hilarious. ___________
5 Dublin, which Mike has lived since he was five, is the capital of Ireland. ___________
6 My friend, which I was following on social media, has blocked me. ___________

Indefinite pronouns

4 Complete the sentences with the correct indefinite pronoun.

1 I don't know *anything* about advertising.
2 My sister deleted ___________ on my computer by accident.
3 There are advertisements for that brand ___________!
4 ___________ at the party was really nice. I had a great time.
5 The teacher wanted ___________ to answer the question, but ___________ knew the answer.
6 Paula says she can't find her glasses ___________.

Reflexive and reciprocal pronouns

5 Complete the conversation with the pronouns in the box.

anything	anywhere	each other	~~everyone~~
himself	nobody	someone	themselves

MIA So how was Phil's party?
NOAH Oh, it was great fun. [1] *Everyone* really enjoyed [2] ___________. And the food was delicious.
MIA Phil's a good cook. Did he make it all [3] ___________?
NOAH Yes, … well he says [4] ___________ helped him, but I think his sister made the cake.
MIA So did [5] ___________ interesting happen?
NOAH Not really … Sam and Katie had had an argument and weren't speaking to [6] ___________. Oh, and Carmen lost her coat and she couldn't find it [7] ___________. It turned out that [8] ___________ had taken it home by mistake!

LANGUAGE REFERENCE

Reported statements

Direct speech	Reported speech
Present simple 'I **want** some new shoes.'	**Past simple** He said (that) he **wanted** some new shoes.
Past simple 'I had a great time'.	**Past perfect** She said (that) she **had had** a great time.
Present perfect 'We**'ve** just **seen** a show about a fire.'	**Past perfect** She said (that) they **had** just **seen** a show about a fire.
Present continuous 'We**'re growing** our own vegetables.'	**Past continuous** He said (that) they **were growing** their own vegetables.
will 'They **will** need to bring a laptop.'	***would*** She said (that) they **would** need to bring a laptop.
can 'You **can** do it.'	***could*** He said (that) I **could** do it.
must 'We **must** buy some bread.'	***had to*** She said (that) we **had to** buy some bread.
have to 'I **have to** wear a uniform.'	***had to*** She said (that) she **had to** wear a uniform.

- When we report somebody's words, we often have to change the verb forms – see the table above for how the verb forms change.
- We often need to change pronouns in reported speech.
  *'**You** have to leave before 11 pm'. – He said (that) **we** had to leave before 11 pm.*

Reported commands

- ***tell* + someone + (*not*) *to* + infinitive**
  Direct speech: 'Stop talking, Bruno!'
  Reported speech: The teacher told Bruno to stop talking.

Reported offers and suggestions

- Offers
  ***offer* + (*not*) *to* + infinitive**
  Direct speech: 'I can carry the bag for you.'
  Reported speech: She offered to carry the bag for me.
- Suggestions
  suggest* + (*not*) + *-ing
  Direct speech: 'Let's take the bus.'
  Reported speech: He suggested taking the bus.
- We use different verbs to report offers and suggestions. Each of these verbs is followed by a specific structure – see above.

Reported questions

- When we report questions, we usually make the same changes to the verb forms, pronouns and time references as when we report statements.
- When we report questions with a *Wh-* word, we don't add an auxiliary verb and the word order is the same as in affirmative sentences.
  He asked me what I'd done at the weekend.
  ~~*He asked me what had I done at the weekend.*~~
  Connor asked when the school trip was.
  ~~*Connor asked when was the school trip.*~~
- When we report *Yes/No* questions, we use ***if***.
  'Did you tell the truth?' – They asked him if he'd told the truth.
- We don't use a question mark when we report questions.
  'Where did you go after school?' – My parents asked me where I'd been after school.

LANGUAGE PRACTICE

Reported statements

1 Write the statements in reported speech.

1 'I don't want to go out for lunch.'
   Alison said (that) she didn't want to go out for lunch.
2 'We won't waste any more time.'
   They told us ______
3 'I can help you to make lunch.'
   Joshua said ______
4 'I haven't bought your Christmas presents yet.'
   Andy said to Amy ______
5 'Heidi's moving to Australia next week.'
   You told me ______

Reported commands

2 Complete the second sentence with two or three words to report the command.

1 'Write an essay about technology.'
   The teacher told me to write an essay about technology.
2 'Don't touch my new car!'
   My dad told ______ touch his new car!
3 'Tell them to keep the noise down.'
   Martha told me ______ to keep the noise down.
4 'Don't say anything to Charlie about the concert.'
   She ______ to say anything to Charlie about the concert.

Reported offers and suggestions

3 Complete the reported requests, suggestions and offers with the correct form of the verbs in the box.

collect ~~correct~~ help not tell switch

1 Helen asked us to correct her essay before she gave it to the teacher.
2 My friend's dad offered ______ us from school.
3 They suggested ______ Thomas what had happened.
4 When did Ethan offer ______ you with your maths exam?
5 Who suggested ______ the computer on and off?

Reported questions

4 Rewrite the questions in reported speech.

1 'Are you going to make the dinner?' Jake asked Chloe.
   Jake asked Chloe if she was going to make the dinner.
2 'What will make you change your mind?' Maria asked me.
   ______
3 'Have you ever been to Vienna?' I asked my friend.
   ______
4 'When is the next exam?' Leah asked the teacher.
   ______
5 'Do you change your mind often?' Jake asked her.
   ______

5 Correct the mistake in each sentence.

1 They asked us ~~could we~~ help them. if we could
2 The teacher asked me why hadn't I done my homework. ______
3 The doctor asked me where it does hurt. ______
4 Paula wanted to know if could she borrow my phone. ______
5 My dad asked me what did happen. ______

6 Complete the second sentence so that it means the same as the first. Use no more than three words.

1 'Shall I look after your bag for you?' Paul asked.
   Paul offered to look after my bag for me.
2 'What time is the next bus?' Sarah asked the man.
   Sarah asked the man what time the next bus ______.
3 'Why don't we go out?' Robyn suggested.
   Robyn suggested ______.
4 'Have you seen my hat?' my aunt asked me.
   My aunt asked me if I ______ her hat.
5 'Don't forget that there's no school tomorrow,' the teacher said.
   The teacher told us ______ that there was no school the next day.

LANGUAGE BANK

UNIT 4

Vocabulary

The five senses

feel feel like look look like smell smell like sound sound like taste taste like touch

Describing texture, sound, taste, etc.

colourful faint rough sharp shiny smelly smooth sour spicy transparent

Language in action

Modals of deduction and possibility
Obligation, prohibition, necessity and advice

Speaking

Everyday English

Bingo!
I give up!
I guess so.
nice and warm/hot, etc.
Sure, why not?

Useful language

Guess again.
Guess what it is / they are.
I guess they must be …
Perhaps it's something (+ adjective)
They're definitely some kind of …

Writing

Useful language

According to …
At the age of …
including …
… is known as …
… was born on … and grew up in.

UNIT 5

Vocabulary

Processes

attract collect communicate connect create deliver develop measure produce solve supply waste

Extreme adjectives

boiling deafening dreadful enormous fascinating freezing gorgeous marvellous stunning terrifying

Language in action

The passive
Question tags and questions with prepositions

Speaking

Everyday English

… and everything
Er, not exactly.
I'd say it was …
Oh, man
Wanna … ?

Useful language

Are you kidding me?
I can't believe you actually …
I find that hard to believe.
Seriously?
You can't be serious.

Writing

Useful language

… deserves to win because …
I'm absolutely certain that …
The highlight of a visit to … is …
the … that impressed me the most was …
Without a doubt …

LANGUAGE BANK

UNIT 6

Vocabulary

Verb collocations with get, take and have

get a lot out of get bored get lost
get on my nerves get to know
have doubts have fun have the chance
take advantage of take an interest in
take pleasure in take risks

Inspiration and challenge

Nouns	**Verbs**
bravery	achieve
challenge	encourage
determination	inspire
obstacle	overcome
opportunity	support

Language in action

First and second conditional
Third conditional

Speaking

Everyday English

Come on!
Good for you!
not really
seriously
You've got to be joking!

Useful language

Encouraging

Don't worry, you'll be fine.
You can do it!
You'll feel really proud afterwards.
You'll never know unless you try.

Responding

That's easy for you to say.
What if … (+ past simple)?

Writing

Useful language

For example … / For instance … / such as …
Furthermore … / On the one hand …
I personally believe (that) …
On the other hand …
In conclusion …

UNIT 7

Vocabulary

Feelings

amused annoyed down eager glad
grateful hopeful hurt insecure
peaceful ridiculous satisfied thrilled

Expressions with heart and mind

be in two minds bear in mind
break someone's heart change your mind
close to your heart cross your mind
have something on your mind learn by heart
make your mind up
put your heart into something

Language in action

Gerunds and infinitives
Subject and object questions

Speaking

Everyday English

a little harsh
Don't mention it.
I swear
stressed out
That's kind of you …

Useful language

I can imagine.
Is there anything I can do to help?
It'll all be OK, you'll see.
That's not very nice.
What's the matter?

Writing

Useful language

It might be better (not) to …
It would definitely help to …
I would recommend … (+ *-ing*)
Whatever you do, don't …
Why don't you suggest … (+ *-ing*)?

LANGUAGE BANK

UNIT 8

Vocabulary

Advertising

ad blocker advert advertise brand buyer influence logo marketing company product review seller slogan

Internet verbs

build up comment on delete follow post shut down subscribe to switch off switch on vlog

Language in action

Defining and non-defining relative clauses
Indefinite, reflexive and reciprocal pronouns

Speaking

Everyday English

handy
I don't have a clue.
no-brainer
What's up?

Useful language

I can't recommend it/them enough!
I don't know where to start!
Is it easy to use?
It's the best thing …
(It) would be ideal for …
You really ought to …

Writing

Useful language

… is included.
It allows you to …
It is designed to be used …
One of its best features is …
The one thing that's missing is …

UNIT 9

Vocabulary

Reporting verbs

admit announce apologise claim complain confirm deny discover insist promise refuse suggest

Adverbs of time and manner

after a while eventually fluently gradually nowadays occasionally patiently regularly secretly surprisingly

Language in action

Reported statements and commands
Reported questions

Speaking

Everyday English

Hey!
Let me guess.
show-off
sort of
to make matters worse

Useful language

Basically, what happened was …
It was so (+ adjective)
So anyway, …
The next thing I knew …
You'll never guess what happened …

Writing

Useful language

An email

A man/woman from …
He/She announced/explained/admitted that …
'…,' he/she said
Surprisingly/Nowadays etc. …
When asked … he/she answered/explained/said …

IRREGULAR VERBS

Infinitive	Past simple	Past participle
be	was/were	been
beat	beat	beaten
become	became	become
begin	began	begun
bite	bit	bitten
blow	blew	blown
break	broke	broken
bring	brought	brought
build	built	built
buy	bought	bought
catch	caught	caught
choose	chose	chosen
come	came	come
cost	cost	cost
cut	cut	cut
do	did	done
draw	drew	drawn
drink	drank	drunk
drive	drove	driven
eat	ate	eaten
fall	fell	fallen
feel	felt	felt
fight	fought	fought
find	found	found
fly	flew	flown
forget	forgot	forgotten
get	got	got
give	gave	given
go	went	gone
grow	grew	grown
hang	hung	hung
have	had	had
hear	heard	heard
hide	hid	hidden
hit	hit	hit
hold	held	held
hurt	hurt	hurt
keep	kept	kept
know	knew	known
leave	left	left
lend	lent	lent

Infinitive	Past simple	Past participle
let	let	let
lie	lied	lied
light	lit	lit
lose	lost	lost
make	made	made
mean	meant	meant
meet	met	met
pay	paid	paid
put	put	put
read	read	read
ride	rode	ridden
ring	rang	rung
rise	rose	risen
run	ran	run
say	said	said
see	saw	seen
sell	sold	sold
send	sent	sent
shine	shone	shone
shoot	shot	shot
show	showed	shown
shut	shut	shut
sing	sang	sung
sit	sat	sat
sleep	slept	slept
speak	spoke	spoken
spend	spent	spent
stand	stood	stood
steal	stole	stolen
swim	swam	swum
take	took	taken
teach	taught	taught
tear	tore	torn
tell	told	told
think	thought	thought
throw	threw	thrown
understand	understood	understood
wake	woke	woken
wear	wore	worn
win	won	won
write	wrote	written

Student's Book acknowledgements

The authors and publishers acknowledge the following sources of copyright material and are grateful for the permissions granted. While every effort has been made, it has not always been possible to identify the sources of all the material used, or to trace all copyright holders. If any omissions are brought to our notice, we will be happy to include the appropriate acknowledgements on reprinting & in the next update to the digital edition, as applicable.

Key: CLIL = Content and Language Integrated Learning, EM = End Matter, U = Unit, VB = Vocabulary Bank.

Photography

The following photographs are sourced from Getty Images.

U5: Satyan Chawla/500px Prime; Elena Pueyo/Moment; Andyworks/iStock/Getty Images Plus; Peter Schaefer/EyeEm; urfinguss/iStock/Getty Images Plus; Fabien_Gouby/iStock/Getty Images Plus; DiyanaDimitrova/iStock/Getty Images Plus; pskeltonphoto/Moment; chombosan/iStock/Getty Images Plus; Kitti Boonnitrod/Moment; HandmadePictures/iStock/Getty Images Plus; Ringo_Wong_hkherper/iStock/Getty Images Plus; Stígur Már Karlsson/Heimsmyndir/E+; DEA PICTURE LIBRARY/De Agostini; NASA/SCIENCE PHOTO LIBRARY; Creative Crop/Photodisc; Robin-Angelo Photography/Moment; Olivia ZZ/Moment; IndiaPictures/Universal Images Group; kajornyot/iStock/Getty Images Plus; kickimages/iStock/Getty Images Plus; Nitish Waila/iStock/Getty Images Plus; Amos Chapple/Lonely Planet Images; Anton Jankovoy/Moment; kdshutterman/iStock/Getty Images Plus; Shin Okamoto/Moment; Dorling Kindersley; mocoo/iStock/Getty Images Plus; **U6:** dennisvdw/iStock/Getty Images Plus; Philip Lee Harvey/The Image Bank; egon69/E+; Noel Hendrickson/DigitalVision; Andersen Ross Photography Inc/DigitalVision; Igor Emmerich/Cultura; Scott Sansenbach - Sansenbach Marine Photo/Moment; Lawrence Lucier/FilmMagic; Blend Images - Erik Isakson; dtiberio/iStock/Getty Images Plus; Juice Images Ltd; SolStock/E+; Frank Wijn/Moment Open; rozelt/iStock/Getty Images Plus; lvcandy/DigitalVision Vectors; mocoo/iStock/Getty Images Plus; **U7:** martin-dm/E+; bestdesigns/iStock/Getty Images Plus; BrianAJackson/iStock/Getty Images Plus; kgtoh/iStock/Getty Images Plus; Spohn Matthieu/PhotoAlto Agency RF Collections; Siphotography/iStock/Getty Images Plus; KatarzynaBialasiewicz/iStock/Getty Images Plus; Maskot; Ismailciydem/iStock/Getty Images Plus; mocoo/iStock/Getty Images Plus; **U8:** Juanmonino/iStock/Getty Images Plus; Hero Images; JohnnyGreig/E+; filo/DigitalVision Vectors; Diy13/iStock/Getty Images Plus; Milkos/iStock/Getty Images Plus; SPL IMAGES/Photographer's Choice; monkeybusinessimages/iStock/Getty Images Plus; photo/iStock/Getty Images Plus; robertiez/iStock/Getty Images Plus; Julian Kreler/EyeEm; mocoo/iStock/Getty Images Plus; **U9:** Hero Images; XiFotos/E+; sarah5/iStock/Getty Images Plus; photosindia; kelly bowden/Moment; chameleonseye/iStock/Getty Images Plus; Westend61; Hero Images; mocoo/iStock/Getty Images Plus; **VB5:** erhui1979/DigitalVision Vectors; RapidEye/E+; Martin Diebel; Vicki Jauron, Babylon and Beyond Photography/Moment; sturti/E+; Marina Malikova/500px; ralucahphotography.ro/Moment; MaximShebeko/iStock/Getty Images Plus; Baac3nes/Moment; Johannes Hulsch/EyeEm Premium; **VB6:** Muhammad Faidz Zainal Abidin/EyeEm; deimagine/E+; BJI/Blue Jean Images; Sam Edwards/Caiaimage; PhotoAlto/Eric Audras/PhotoAlto Agency RF Collections; digitalskillet/iStock/Getty Images Plus; Chris Whitehead/Cultura; Caiaimage/Martin Barraud; Ricardo Lim/Moment Unreleased; Indeed; **VB7:** Plume Creative/DigitalVision; MediaProduction/E+; Elva Etienne/Moment; Mordolff/E+; Mint Images - Tim Robbins; Jose Luis Pelaez Inc/DigitalVision; xavierarnau/E+; Daisy-Daisy/iStock/Getty Images Plus; Emilija Manevska/Moment; slavemotion/E+; Paul Bradbury/OJO Images; Tom Merton/Caiaimage; moodboard/Cultura; **VB8:** littleny/iStock Editorial/Getty Images Plus; **VB9:** mikroman6/Moment; Maskot; **CLIL6:** SeventyFour/iStock/Getty Images Plus; **CLIL8:** paseven/iStock/Getty Images Plus.

The following photographs are sourced from other source.

ICONS: Prithvi/Noun Project; Agni/Noun Project; mikicon/Noun Project; Baboon designs, US/Noun Project; Tanguy Keryhuel, FR/Noun Project; Icons Bazaar/Noun Project; Adrien Coquet, FR/Noun Project; Vectors Market/Noun Project; TukTuk Design/Noun Project; iconsphere, ID/Noun Project; i cons, US/Noun Project; kim Eriksson/Noun Project; Lloyd Humphreys, DK/Noun Project; Delwar Hossain, BD/Noun Project; Kirby Wu, TW/Noun Project; Magicon, HU/Noun Project; Baboon designs, US/Noun Project.

Illustrations

U8, U9, EM: Claire Rollet (Illustration Web); **U5:** Sean Longcroft.

Video Stills

The following stills are sourced from Getty Images.

U5: Schroptschop/Creatas Video; dottedhippo/iStock/Getty Images Plus; Barry Kusuma/DigitalVision; **U6:** helivideo/Creatas Video+/Getty Images Plus; Hill Street Studios/DigitalVision; © Randy Faris/Corbis/VCG; **U7:** Rost-9D/Creatas Video+/Getty Images Plus; urbazon/E+; Jose Luis Pelaez Inc/DigitalVision; silverkblack/Creatas Video+/Getty Images Plus; **U8:** Stusya/Creatas Video+/Getty Images Plus; Kevin Dodge; LeoPatrizi/E+; **U9:** FilmColoratStudio/Vetta; Karl Weatherly/Photographer's Choice; Eastfootage/Image Bank Film.

The following stills are sourced from other source.

S5–U9: Lucentum Digital.

Cover design and illustrations: Collaborate Agency.

Video produced by Lucentum Digital.

Audio produced by Creative Listening.

Typeset by Blooberry Design.